A DESCRIPTION OF NEW NETHERLAND

The Iroquoians and
Their World

EDITORS
José António Brandão
William A. Starna

A DESCRIPTION OF NEW NETHERLAND

ADRIAEN VAN DER DONCK

Edited by Charles T. Gehring and William A. Starna

Translated by Diederik Willem Goedhuys | Foreword
by Russell Shorto

University of Nebraska Press | Lincoln and London

Map on page xxiv courtesy of
New York State Library.

Library of Congress
Cataloging-in-Publication Data
Donck, Adriaen van der, 1620–1655.
[Beschryvinge van Nieuvv-Nederlant. English]
A description of New Netherland / Adriaen
van der Donck; edited by Charles T.
Gehring and William A. Starna; translated
by Diederik Willem Goedhuys; foreword by
Russell Shorto.
p. cm. — (The Iroquoians and their world)
Includes bibliographical references and index.
ISBN 978-0-8032-1088-2 (cloth: alk. paper)
ISBN 978-0-8032-3283-9 (paper: alk. paper)
1. New York (State)—Description and
travel—Early works to 1800. 2. New York
(State)—History—Colonial period, ca.
1600–1775. 3. New Netherland—Description
and travel. 4. New Netherland—History.
5. Dutch—New York (State)—History—17th
century. 6. Indians of North America—New
York (State)—History—17th century.
7. West-Indische Compagnie (Netherlands)—
History—17th century. I. Gehring, Charles T.,
1939– II. Starna, William A. III. Goedhuys,
D. W. (Diederik Willem) IV. Title.
F122.1.D6613 2008   974.7′02—dc22
2008013584

Set in Adobe Caslon Pro.
Designed by A. Shahan.

CONTENTS

A DESCRIPTION OF NEW NETHERLAND:

73 **Of the Manners and Extraordinary Qualities of the Original Natives of New Netherland**

FOREWORD

Russell Shorto

In 1641 a young Dutchman did what millions of Europeans after him would do: left his home and all that he knew and set off on a voyage to America. Of those millions, most would live fairly anonymous lives; a few would do great things and receive due attention in history books. Adriaen van der Donck—who was born, probably in 1618, in the Dutch city of Breda, and died in 1655, most likely at his estate along the Hudson River—falls in between: his achievements in his adopted homeland are remarkable, and yet he has been largely forgotten.

This publication is in part an attempt at redressing that oversight. Van der Donck's *A Description of New Netherland* was published in full exactly twice—in 1655 and 1656—both times in Dutch. There was one incomplete English translation, done in 1841 and reprinted in 1968, which scholars have long realized is inadequate. Besides its inaccuracies, that version left out some of the best and most historically important parts of the book, including much of Van der Donck's noteworthy account of the region's Indians. The historian Thomas O'Donnell called *A Description of New Netherland* "one of America's oldest literary treasures" and said that were it not for the fact that Van der Donck wrote in Dutch rather than English, "his *Description* would certainly have won from posterity the same kind, if not the same amount, of veneration that has been bestowed on Bradford's *Of Plymouth Plantation*."

That is a strong statement—William Bradford's book is our main source on the Pilgrims and thus the key to our understanding of the settlers whom Samuel Eliot Morison called the "spiritual ancestors of all Americans"—and yet it seems justified. To appreciate both what Van der Donck did and why he was forgotten, one must reconfigure the commonly accepted way of thinking about American beginnings. Textbooks often portray American history as beginning with thirteen English colonies: to imagining it as an English root onto which, over time, other cultures would be grafted to create the famed American "melting pot." There is no sense in denying that the English became the dominant European settlers of America. But emphasizing the early settlements in New England and Virginia has meant largely overlooking the vast stretch of the North American coast between these two regions.

This region—encompassing all or parts of the future states of New York, New Jersey, Connecticut, Pennsylvania, and Delaware—constituted the colony of New Netherland, which the Dutch founded following Henry Hudson's 1609 voyage to North America. Hudson was an English mariner and explorer, but for his most historically significant journey he happened to sail for the Dutch East India Company, thus allowing the Dutch to claim the territory he had navigated. While the English colonies at Jamestown, Plymouth, and Massachusetts Bay were developing, the settlers of New Netherland were doing much the same as their English counterparts: laying roads, building brick houses, setting up courts, marrying, giving birth, and dying.

From the beginning, the colony existed under the auspices of the Dutch West India Company, whose directors had a narrow vision of it, as a thing to be exploited for profit. The settlers, however, quickly developed different ideas. The clash between their interests and those of the company came to a climax when Willem Kieft, the colony's director from 1638 to 1647, declared war on the Indians in the vicinity of Manhattan. The colonists saw this as doubly disastrous: not only were they vastly outnumbered by the Indians, but they were also there to do business with them. The Europeans had come as fur traders, and they depended on the Indians to supply pelts. As the colonists feared, the brutal attacks that Kieft's soldiers unleashed on Indian villages were countered by the natives' bloody assaults at New Amsterdam and elsewhere. The settlers retreated into the safety of the fort and pondered how they would salvage their future.

Enter Adriaen van der Donck. He had come to the New World colony in August 1641, fresh from the University of Leiden, the premier educational institution in the United Provinces, where he had studied law. The law faculty at the university was at this time under the modernizing influence of the great Hugo de Groot, a.k.a. Grotius, who has gone down in history as the father of international law. More generally, Dutch universities in the 1630s were experiencing the first impact of the thinking of Galileo and Descartes, who proposed to reorient all knowledge. No longer would Aristotle and the Bible stand as the sole bases on which inquiry rested. Instead, the human mind, with its "good sense," as Descartes said, would be the arbiter of truth.

These were heady days in which to get a university education—stirrings of talk about what we would call democracy, human rights, and the rights of women were in the air. Judging from what Van der Donck would soon do, it seems fair to say that he had a desire to put what he had learned into practice. A safe, comfortable position in the Dutch Republic might have made sense: the nation was in the midst of its golden age, and legal work for a smart young man with the very best training would have been readily available. But Van der Donck opted for something else. An Amsterdam diamond merchant named Kiliaen van Rensselaer had been granted the right of a patroonship within the colony of New Netherland in 1629. Called Rensselaerswijck, the land extended to both sides of the northern end of the Hudson River and encircled the West India Company's Fort Orange. He planned for the patroonship to become a for-profit farming community and in 1630 started peopling the area. Over the following years he shipped farmers, carpenters, wheelwrights, and others to join in his New World venture. To keep the peace he needed to fill the vacated position of *schout*, a Dutch office that combined the roles of law enforcement officer and prosecuting attorney. Van der Donck applied for the job and was accepted.

But after three years dispensing justice for Van Rensselaer, Van der Donck shifted his attention further south, to the trouble brewing on Manhattan. He joined the community and at once was drawn into the center of the conflict between the West India Company director and the inhabitants. He became at once a political organizer and the legal counsel of the settlers. He crafted a lengthy series of formal legal petitions and complaints on their behalf, which were sent either to the West India Company or directly to the seat of Dutch government in the Hague. These decried the ill treatment of the settlers and demanded justice. They made an appeal that the management of the colony be taken over by the government.

In large part due to these complaints, the West India Company decided to replace Willem Kieft. His successor, Petrus Stuyvesant, would become an admirable foil to Van der Donck. Indeed, the two men seem to represent two different temperaments not only of Dutchmen but of Europeans in the seventeenth century. Van der Donck had a humanistic training, while Stuyvesant was the son of a Calvinist minister from Friesland, who had grown up in the service of the West India Company. Stuyvesant arrived on Manhattan in the spring of

1647 intent on quelling the rebellion among certain colonists and imposing proper order. Van der Donck and his allies, meanwhile, were only beginning their opposition. Stuyvesant had barely settled into the fort when the citizens presented him with a long list of "interrogatories," which were meant as part of an appeal for a reorganization of the colony. Stuyvesant reacted with outrage, at which Van der Donck responded with an even more strident demand that the case of the colony be brought before the government. "Let us then once see what the law of nations thinks of it," his letter concluded, employing a phrase straight out of Grotius.

At the height of these tensions, Stuyvesant ordered Van der Donck put under house arrest and even threatened to have him executed for treason. His council urged him to release the man, however, and shortly thereafter Van der Donck sailed back to the United Provinces as part of a three-man delegation. Their goal was to bring the cause of New Netherland directly to the States General, the Dutch governing body. What the colonists wanted was a form of representative government, and they had chosen a prime moment to demand it. In the preceding year, 1648, the Dutch Republic's Eighty Years' War with Spain had come to an end, at the same time that the wider Thirty Years' War was settled. The spirit of Grotius hung over the peace treaties and with it a radical new approach to political thought based on a belief in the rational behavior of sovereign states.

The Dutch government delayed its response to the petition of the New Netherlanders, but Van der Donck remained active. During the hiatus he published a map of the northeast coast of North America, which would become the standard representation of the area for more than a century, and which would imprint Dutch placenames—from "Rhoode Eylandt" to Cape May—permanently on the American landscape. He also had the formal complaint published. It appeared under the title *Remonstrance of New Netherland, Concerning Its Location, Fruitfulness, and Sorry Condition*. Through it Dutchmen came to learn of the vigorous but mismanaged colony of New Netherland, of the Dutch presence in America, and of the island called Manhattan. People began clamoring to emigrate. The directors of the West India Company were bewildered. "Formerly New Netherland was never spoken of, and now heaven and earth seem to be stirred up by it," they wrote in a letter to Stuyvesant.

Finally, in this moment of new ideas and new possibilities in the wake of the treaties of 1648, Van der Donck's petition succeeded. The States General ruled that the government could no longer "approve of the perverse administration of the privileges and benefits granted by charter to the stockholders of the West India Company [while] neglecting or opposing the good plans and offers submitted for the security of the boundaries and the increase of the population of that country." The government awarded New Amsterdam a municipal charter: henceforth, this city an ocean away, surrounded by unexplored lands and unfamiliar Native peoples, would be considered an actual Dutch municipality. The government further authorized the conveyance of settlers to Manhattan. And Petrus Stuyvesant was recalled.

Van der Donck scarcely had time to revel in his victory, however, before disaster struck. Rumors of war with England suddenly consumed the government; when the First Anglo-Dutch War was declared in July 1652, it spelled the end of Van der Donck's mission. The Dutch leaders were not about to experiment with political reform at a time of crisis. They rescinded their provisional ruling.

Van der Donck was bereft, victory snatched from him. Not only was the order to recall Stuyvesant rescinded; Van der Donck was forbidden to return to Manhattan. But he did not stay idle. Van der Donck's passion was not purely political. Under the West India Company's mismanagement, New Netherland had languished, while the populations of the New England colonies were growing rapidly. Moreover, in his years as *schout* of Rensselaerswijck he had roamed the country, spent time among the Indians, and heard stories about the staggering size of the continent. When he made his appeal before the government leaders, he stressed the historic opportunity that the colony represented. Now he wanted to find a way to let more Dutchmen know of the colony. He put pen to paper and wrote a book into which he poured every fact about his adopted home that he could summon. He wrote of its rivers, its mountains, the Indians and their way of life. He cataloged the plants, the types of fruit, the character of the seasons, and the varieties of animal species. At the end, in the manner of the time, he constructed a dialogue between a Dutchman and a New Netherland settler, in which the Dutchman poses naive but interested questions about the colony. Here Van der Donck became something of a prophet, for in his answers the New Netherlander talks of the scope and potential of the new land. Because of what it offers and the fact that the Dutch Republic has been a haven for refugees from all over Europe, he says, this new colony will one day rise in power to outstrip the home country. People from across Europe will flock to New Netherland. There they will enjoy the New World's abundance and make a new home.

This book, with its lively passion for America and its prophetic tone, was *A Description of New Netherland*. Its depictions of North America at mid-seventeenth century are intoxicating even—especially—today. It is a raw and rough classic, a window into what once was and is now lost forever. And it is a work of ironic prophecy, for all that Van der Donck predicted would come to pass, but it would happen under the auspices not of the Dutch but of the English.

Van der Donck was eventually allowed to sail back to New

Netherland. He returned to his estate along the Hudson River, just north of Manhattan. There, in 1655, probably in a general Indian attack on the whole region, he met his death. The exact date of his birth is uncertain, but most likely he died at the age of thirty-seven. Because he was referred to by the Dutch title of Jonkheer—something akin to "young squire"—his property would in later years become known as the Jonkheer's land, and then simply Yonkers, so the city of that name in Westchester County, New York, is his one tangible legacy.

But there are others, less obvious but greater. Although Van der Donck did not see his full plan for the colony enacted, one part of it was carried out. Because of him the city of New Amsterdam received a municipal charter. This would help cement features of the Dutch system into it, so that, after the English takeover of the colony in 1664, these features—notably a commitment to free trade—would remain a part of the new city of New York. They would mold the city as it evolved, and through it they would have an even broader influence through the centuries. When people use phrases like "melting pot" and "cultural diversity," they often suppose them to be twentieth-century notions. In fact, they have a much older heritage. Adriaen van der Donck has been dead for three and a half centuries, but some people have a way of living on, even when they are forgotten. Van der Donck's legacy is still with us. As he says himself in this new English translation of the complete work, "A territory like New Netherland . . . must it not, given appropriate initiatives and direction, eventually prosper?—Judge for yourself."

PREFACE

Charles T. Gehring and William A. Starna

In a perfect world there would be no need for translators or their translations. However, acknowledging our imperfect state, we must be prepared to deal not only with thousands of languages but also with the various historical stages in the development of these languages and their dialects. For historic texts such as Adriaen van der Donck's *A Description of New Netherland*, a translator needs to be familiar with both the subtleties of a language spoken and written four hundred years ago and, of course, its particular cultural and social contexts. Absent such knowledge a translator can only produce a literal translation devoid of the original's linguistic nuances and sense of time and place. In this situation, then, a translator perforce resorts to the mechanical process of translating word for word—often with the assistance of rudimentary reference materials—reducing complex thoughts to inaccurate depictions or silently eliminating troublesome words, phrases, and even entire clauses. The translation of Van der Donck's *Description* by Jeremiah Johnson in 1841 falls into this category.

It has been known for many years that Johnson's translation was defective, as the introduction to the most recent reprint of his work concedes: "Johnson was not a professional writer, and his translation is not consistently graceful. He seems to have had difficulty with certain seventeenth century Dutch constructions—particularly reflexives and other pronouns. *A Description* probably deserves and may some day get a more polished translation; but the fact remains that Johnson's is still the only one in print."[1] Not to belabor the point, one example, demonstrating why a new translation is needed, should suffice. In the opening pages of his work Van der Donck offers brief details contrasting certain Dutch physical features with those of the Native people of New Netherland, writing, "Op de borst ende omtrendt den mont gantsch kael / ende den Vrouwen ghelijckt / de onse heel hayrigh." Johnson translates this passage thus: "Their men on the breast and about the mouth were bare, and their women like ours, hairy." Diederik Goedhuys correctly translates the same passage: "The Indian men are entirely bald on the chest and around the mouth like women; ours, quite hairy." Such errors abound in the Johnson translation, as the assessment by Dutch scholar Ada van Gastel made clear nearly two decades ago.[2]

As important as it is that the translator do justice to the original language, it is also critical that the text be placed in its appropriate cultural context. We have attempted to do so by annotating Van der Donck's treatise, providing readers with historical, ethnological, and linguistic information of special note and, where necessary, clarifying observations on natural history. We also offer comment on Dutch and English-language literature relating to the New World, in particular New England and New Netherland, that Van der Donck had at his disposal as an educated person of the mid-seventeenth century. As it was then common for writers to "borrow" observations from other published work, we have suggested possible sources of this information. It should also be noted that Van der Donck wrote in a highly educated style, full of complex constructions, contemporary metaphors, and historical allusions. It is the translator's challenge to approach the original with the closest equivalent in the target language.

Where Johnson failed, Goedhuys succeeded. But Johnson's failings were caused more by the paucity of reference works available to him in the nineteenth century than by his intellectual abilities. Without access to the massive Dutch dictionary—*Woordenboek der Nederlandsche Taal* (1888–1998)—with its extensive historical definitions in contexts from printed sources going back to the sixteenth century, the translator is left to fly blind, assisted by only very basic dictionaries with their one-to-one correspondences in contemporary usages. It is impressive that translators in the nineteenth century, such as Johnson, were able to translate as well as they did with what they had at their disposal. Diederik Goedhuys, on the other hand, was able to work on this new translation for a summer at the New Netherland Project, where he had access to every possible reference source available for the translation of a seventeenth-century publication. In addition to the *Woordenboek* and the reference collection of the New York State Library, he could examine original copies of both editions of Van der Donck's *Description*. Goedhuys also has the advantage of being a native of the Netherlands who has spent over thirty years in South Africa. His familiarity with the development of the Dutch language and culture in a foreign environment, such as South Africa, can only be considered a benefit for the translation of Van der Donck's work.

Finally, it should be noted that the editors have made only minor adjustments to Goedhuys's translation; for example, the noun *wild/wilt*, which literally translates in the singular as "wild one," will appear in this translation as "Indian," not as "savage." Numbers in the margin indicate the page number in the original.

PUBLICATION HISTORY OF
ADRIAEN VAN DER DONCK'S
A Description of New Netherland

1655: Adriaen van der Donck, *Beschryvinge van Nieuvv Nederlant, (ghelijck het tegenwoordigh in staet is) begrijpende de nature, aert, gelegentheyt en vrucht-baerheyt van het selve lant; mitsgaders de proffijte-lijcke ende gewenste toevallen, die aldaer tot onderhout der menschen, (soo uyt haer selven als van buyten ingebracht) gevonden worden. Als mede De maniere en onghemeyne eygenschappen vande wilden oste naturellen vanden lande. Enge een bysonder verhael vanden wonderlijcken aert ende het weesen der bevers, daer noch by gevoeght is een discours over de gelegentheyt van Nieuw Nederlandt, tusschen een Nederlandt patriot, ende een Nieuw Nederlander* (T'Aemsteldam [The Netherlands]: Evert Nieuwenhof).

1656: Adriaen van der Donck, *Beschryvinge van Nieuvv-Nederlant, (gelijck het tegenwoordigh in staet is) begrijpende de nature, aert, gelegentheyt en vruchtbaerheyt van het selve landt.* . . . *Daer noch by-gevoeght is een Discours over de gelegentheyt van Nieuw-Nederlandt, tusschen een Nederlandts patriot, ende een Nieuw Nederlander* (T'Aemsteldam [The Netherlands]: Evert Nieuwenhof).

1841: [Adriaen van der Donck,] *"Description of New Netherlands,* by Adriaen van der Donck, J. U. D., translated from the

xxi

original Dutch by Hon. Jeremiah Johnson," in *Collections of the New York Historical Society*, 2nd ser., vol. 1, pt. 5, 125–242 (New York: New York Historical Society).

1896: Adriaen van der Donck, *Description of New Netherland*, trans. Jeremiah Johnson, Old South Leaflets, vol. 4, no. 69 (Boston: Directors of the Old South Work).

1968: Adriaen van der Donck, *A Description of the New Netherlands*, ed. Thomas F. O'Donnell (Syracuse NY: Syracuse University Press).

A DESCRIPTION OF NEW NETHERLAND

MAP OF NEW NETHERLAND

THE COUNTRY

Where New Netherland Is Situated

New Netherland, thus named by the Dutch for reasons we shall give hereafter, is a very beautiful, pleasant, healthy, and delightful land, where all manner of men can more easily earn a good living and make their way in the world than in the Netherlands or any other part of the globe that I know.

It is situated in the northern regions of the new American world and extends along the coast from 38°53′ north of the equator to beyond 42° north. Those are the latitudes of Sardinia and Corsica in the Mediterranean Sea, and of Spain and France on the [Atlantic] Ocean, for the South River [Delaware River] corresponds with the Flemish islands at one end and the river of Lisbon [Tagus River] and the southernmost point of Sardinia at the other. Reckoned from the longitude of the Canary Islands, New Netherland lies at 316° east or 44° west, a distance of 660 miles at the latitude of Cape Misurata on the Barbary Coast of Africa in the Kingdom of Tripoli, and of Cape Spartivento at the extremity of Italy in the Mediterranean Sea.[1]

When and by Whom New Netherland Was First Discovered

This country was first discovered in the year of our Lord Jesus Christ 1609, when the ship *Halve Maen* was dispatched at the expense of the chartered East India Company to seek a westerly passage to the Kingdom of China.[2] The captain and supercargo of this ship was one Henry Hudson, who, though of English birth, had long lived among the Dutch and was then in the service and pay of the East India Company. Steering a course west by north from the Canary Islands and making fair progress for twenty days, the ship encountered land at an estimated 320° west. They saw no sign that Christians had ever been there before, so that the country had now been newly discovered. Approaching, they found the coast and beach suitable for landing, went ashore, and surveyed and took possession of the land as best they could under the circumstances.

Why This Territory Was Named New Netherland

As we have heard, the Dutch discovered and took possession of this country in the year 1609. In fertility, equable climate, opportunity for trade, seaports, watercourses, fisheries, weather, and wind, and whatever other commendable qualities one may care to mention, it is so similar to the Netherlands or, truth to say, generally superior to it, that for good reasons they named it New Netherland, that is, another and newfound Netherlands. Yet it is the first discovery that usually counts, and the similarity of climate or temperature mattered rather less to others.

We observe that the French named their possessions in the same part of the New World Canada, or Nova Francia, solely because they took them first, for the climate or temperature is not like that of France at all. France tends to be warm rather than cold, and New France is so cold and wintry that snow commonly covers the country for four or five months on end, often four or five feet deep, so that keeping European cattle there comes very expensive. Even though the country extends no farther north than 50°, its winter air is so thin, clear, and crisp that snow, which normally falls from late November or December, does not thaw again except through the force of the sun, usually in April. It seldom rains in winter, for the cold air is dry rather than humid, but if it does, the snow subsides somewhat and a hard crust forms on top, which makes for heavy going across country for man and beast, and it rarely melts and disappears all at once.

Likewise the Swedes have a settlement there they call New Sweden, which differs altogether from Sweden in climate or temperature, being situated below our territory at 39° north, yet they pretend to call it so because they own some land there. Their title to it is much disputed, and they would not be able to prove its legality.[3]

So New Netherland, having been first discovered by the Dutch, was thus named, also in view of that discovery. That this country was first found by the Dutch also appears clearly from what the many Indians, or natives, still living there and old enough to remember told us freely on various occasions: Before the arrival of the Dutch ship *Halve Maen* in 1609, they did not know there were more people in the world than those of their kind around them, much less people so different in type and appearance as their nation is from ours. The Indian men are entirely hairless on the chest and around the mouth like women; ours, quite hairy. They wear no clothes and mostly no headgear, especially in summer, and we are always clothed and covered.

When some of them first saw our ship approaching in the distance, they knew not what to make of it and dreaded that it be a ghostly or similar apparition from heaven or from hell; others wondered whether it might be a rare fish or a sea monster, and those on board devils or humans, and so on, each according to his inclination. Strange reports of the event were current in the country at the time and caused great despondency among the Indians, as several of them have declared to me more than once. This we take as certain proof that the Dutch were the first finders and possessors of New Netherland. Because there are Indians whose memories go back more than a hundred years and who, if others had been there before us, [they] would have made mention of it, and if they had not seen these themselves, would at least have heard of it from their ancestors.[4]

Some believe that the Spaniards visited this country many years ago but finding it too cold to their liking left again. Beans and Turkish corn, or maize, are thought to have remained among the Indians from that time, but this is improbable and I have never heard as much from the Indians. They say that beans and corn came to them from the southern Indians who had earlier obtained them from people living still farther south. That may well be true, for Castilians have long been living in Florida. Or perhaps corn had been known before by the Indians in the warm parts of the country; our Indians say that before they knew of corn they ate tree bark or roots instead of bread.[5]

---

4   **The Dutch, the First Possessors of New Netherland**

Though the possession and title held by the Dutch to New Netherland were treated at length in the *Remonstrance*, and little more could be said unless one had the records of the honorable West India Company at his disposal, we shall touch on the matter in passing.[6]

When the Dutch first made a landfall here in 1609, then, and learned from the natives that they were the first Christians and discoverers, they took possession of the land in the name and on behalf of their excellencies the States General of the United Netherlands, first on the South Bay [Delaware Bay] at Cape Henlopen, which is the name they gave to it and which it still bears.[7] They then sailed up the coast, naming the places on the rivers, as far as the great North River, which they ascended quite far. The English prefer to call it the Hudson River, but the Dutch at that time named it the Mauritius River after Prince Maurits, the then governor of the Netherlands. From there they sailed on past Cape Cod, of which they also took possession, naming it New Holland.

The Dutch have since then called and traded continually at the places thus acquired, and when the charter of the West India Company was granted, this territory was included in it. Although we had some places with fortifications, settlers, and livestock there before then, since 1622 several forts, farms, and plantations have been established. Also, many tracts of land were purchased from the natives and other evidence of possession given from time to time, as is shown at length in the above-mentioned *Remonstrance* of the community of New Netherland, to which we refer the interested reader. Therefore it is very odd, improper, and unreasonable for any other nation to presume to have any title to or jurisdiction in this place or others included with it, since it has been from the first a Dutch possession.

The Limits of New Netherland and How Far They Extend

New Netherland is bounded by the ocean separating Europe from America, by New England, the river of Canada [St. Lawrence River] or New France—though only in part—and Virginia. Some less-informed people refer to the whole of North America by the name of Virginia, because Virginia is well known for the tobacco trade that is prominent there; we merely alert the reader to this before we proceed.

The coast of New Netherland runs generally, with local deviations, from southwest to northeast. The shore is for the most part clean and sandy, and water drains off well. To the southwest the country borders on Virginia; the boundary line is yet to be determined, but as the population grows there ought to be little or no difficulty on that score. On the northeast New Netherland abuts on New England. The boundary is not un-disputed, and we could wish that the matter were settled. To the north the river of Canada extends over a great distance, but the northwestern limit is not yet known or defined.

Several of our people have penetrated far into the country to at least seventy or eighty miles from the coastline. We of-ten trade with Indians from parts ten, twenty, or more days' travel inland who have been hunting beavers still farther out, but they are not aware of any end, limit, or boundary, and appear amazed when questioned concerning it. Therefore we may safely say that the full extent of the country is not known, though there are indications, such as the prevailing wind from landward, the severe cold, the multitude of beavers and other game being caught, and the passage and return of great flocks of waterfowl, that the land stretches for hundreds of miles into the interior, so that the size of this province is as yet unknown.

Of the Coast, Foreshore, and Seaports

The coast of New Netherland, as mentioned above, runs from southwest to northeast, is clean and sandy, drains naturally, and even though exposed to open shallow sea, offers anchor-age most everywhere. This is because the sea bottom is of pure sand, and also because heavy weather seldom comes from the direction of the sea, except sometimes from the southeast at spring tide. With north or northwest wind, which can be very dominant, the shore is to the windward and offers good berthing with little danger. Thus the coast is as convenient and pleasant for landing in all seasons as could be wished, for the uplands are high and visible from afar. The beach drains naturally, giving early warning of nearby land.

The foreshore is mostly double and at some points broken into islands, very suitable for keeping pigs and other cattle. At first sight it appears to be mainland, but the coast actually consists of islands or barrier beaches, beyond which lie spacious marshes, waterways, and creeks, many of them navigable and affording convenient passage from one place to another.

Against the onrush and force of the sea, which might be feared at any time to engulf or wash away coastal land by flooding, storms, or otherwise, nature has most providently taken precaution, for it has pleased God to protect and secure the coastal areas as well as the sand flats, beach, and marshes with firm stone foundations, not everywhere, but in the places where the sea is violent and runs strongly, so that numbers of stone heads line the seaboard of that country, so solid, strong, and high, so appropriate and requisite, as could only with difficulty be fashioned by man at great expense.

The harbors of New Netherland are many and varied, and to describe them all in detail would by itself make a much larger book than we propose this to be. We shall note a few selected features of them so as to leave scope and work for seafaring folk. Starting from the south, then, and ending at Long Island, the first to come into view is Godyns Bay, or South Bay, which was the first to be discovered. It is situated at about 39° north, is six miles wide and nine miles long, and has several sandbars, but is still a good anchorage and safe haven for a great many ships, having space and width enough to harbor them. It is also a good area for catching whales, numbers of which come to the bay in winter to scour themselves on the tidal flats and bars. They are not as fat as the Greenland whales, but there are many to be had, so that the catch would be profitable and show much success if there were a properly equipped settlement in this vicinity. Nine miles farther on, the bay finally narrows into a river that we call the South River, to be more fully discussed later.

We now ought to proceed to the bay into which both the

East and the North rivers flow and where Staten Island is situated. Since it is the most frequented and populated area, and most of the commerce and trade is conducted in and across it, and it also lies in the center of New Netherland, it is preeminently known as The Bay [New York Bay]. Before we speak of it, though, we shall first say a few words concerning the nature of the country between this bay and the South Bay.

Between these two bays the foreshore is mostly a continuous double strip formed by several islands, in some places two or three between the shore and the sea. The foreshore as well as the islands are all well situated and suitable for both coastal villages for various kinds of fishermen and for growing grain, wines, fruit, and vegetables and keeping cattle, as the soil is fertile and fairly heavy and overgrown with trees, vines, plums, hazelnuts, grass, and strawberries. They are also rich in oysters owing to the many oyster beds around and near them.

The many islands, some fairly high, have fine natural bays and harbors, but there are also other convenient inlets for those who know them, as yet little used by shipping, chiefly, the Beeregat, the Great and the Little Egg harbors, the Barnegat [Barnegat Bay], etc., affording very safe and secure berthing. Since New Netherland is not yet as fully occupied and inhabited as could be wished, however, and very few Christians live in or near those places, these facilities are seldom availed of other than in bad weather.

The above-mentioned bay containing Staten Island is all the more famous because the East River and the North River, two fine rivers to be described later, both empty into it, as do several streams, inlets, and creeks, some resembling small rivers and being navigable, such as the Raritans Kil [Raritan River], the Kil van Col, the Newesinck [Navesink River], etc. A further reason for its fame is that this bay can easily provide berthing protected from all dangerous winds to more than a thousand cargo ships, and all of that inland. The entrance to the bay is reasonably wide and free of risk and easy to find for those who have been there before or have been given instructions. If desired and the wind cooperates, it is often quite feasible to sail on one tide from the open sea right up to the city of New Amsterdam, five miles inland, in fully laden ships however big and heavy, and similarly return from New Amsterdam seaward. Usually, however, when sailing out to sea, a course is set below Staten Island to a watering place to take in sufficient water and wood for the last time, both being plentiful there. Or one sails far down the bay behind Sandy Hook to take advantage of wind and tide and await the last passengers with the mail.

Along the sea side of Long Island are also some inlets and spaces for berthing vessels, but they are rarely frequented by our people. The island has some very big inland stretches of water and marshes from which one could reach the sea at high tide; at other times they are too shallow. If the area were populated, some considerable settlements would be seen there, but for the sake of brevity we shall move on.

Between Long Island and the mainland much good berthing is available throughout for small and big ships of all kinds, for while some even regard the whole river itself as a bay, there are many good and convenient bays, harbors, and creeks both on the mainland and on the island opposite, more than are known to us in detail.[8] Most of these have been annexed by the English by various means, as was told in the *Remonstrance* of the commonalty of New Netherland, and hence we leave the matter there and let sleeping dogs lie, and proceed to a description of the principal rivers, streams, and waterways.

The South River

The right of the Dutch to the South River and how they acquired it has been adequately demonstrated in the *Remonstrance* of New Netherland and therefore need not be recounted at length here. It is the site where the ship's company of the *Halve Maen* first took possession of the land before any Christian had ever been there, where we erected our forts, laid out farms, and traded for many years on end, unmolested and free of intervention by anyone until, as a result of misguided policies as shown in the said *Remonstrance*, a number of Dutch Swedes also joined the settlement.[9]

As to a description of the river, we confess to being unable to do justice to its worth and condition. Besides its considerable trade and commerce, which are not to be despised, the river has fourteen navigable inlets and streams. Some are very big and remain sailable far upstream, and may thus be regarded as rivers. The regular tide runs up and freshens these for some miles, to varying extent, and all are fairly broad and deep and have tributaries of their own. This river system and the many rich, fertile fields served by it are well suited for establishing sizable settlements, villages, and towns. The river is spacious and broad, clear and deep, not muddy or weed clogged, and suitable everywhere for mooring and anchoring. The tides are strong and flow up to near the falls.[10] Fine, level land extends on both sides, not too high, though above the water level and the flood tide, excepting some reed beds and marshes. Above the falls the river divides into two large, navigable streams, which continue very far to unknown territory. The river contains several beautiful islands and has many other splendid features. Well-traveled observers rank this river with the most attractive anywhere and compare it to the superb Amazon River, not so much for its size as for the other outstanding qualities of the river and the surrounding countryside. Therefore it would be sad to see such a gem stripped from our hands by foreigners.

Of the North River

The naming of this river [the Hudson River], the title to it, the population of these parts, and other aspects were somewhat discussed in the *Remonstrance*, as well as more fully in a tract that was recently published, or is about to be, so that we can be brief and say simply that, at present, the river is the most renowned and its environs the most populous of any in New Netherland, as several settlements and the city of New Amsterdam on Manhattan Island are situated along its banks. The river carries most of the trade and commerce, the tide runs as far as forty miles upstream, and several fine streams flow into it, including the Little and the Great [Roundout and Esopus creeks], Kats Kil [Catskill Creek], Slapershaven ["Sleepers Harbor," present Sleepy Hollow, i.e., Pocantico River], Colendoncks-kil or Sagh-kil [Bronx River], the Wappinckes-kil [Wappingers Creek], etc. From the North River one can sail behind Manhattan Island and reach New England via the East River without approaching New Amsterdam. The river is still entirely under Dutch control and has not been invaded, but were the population not to increase, continued possession would be in great danger. The river is rich in fish, such as sturgeon, rockfish, black bass, and sheepshead. I cannot refrain from relating here, though I digress somewhat, that in March 1647, when a strong ice flow from above had made the river fresh as far as the sea—at normal tide, fresh water comes down to twenty or twenty-four miles from the sea—two fairly big whales swam more than forty miles up the river.[11] One turned back and became stranded, later freeing itself at a spot eleven or twelve miles from the sea where four others were stranded in the same year; the other beached itself not far from the great Cohoes Falls, forty-three miles from the sea. The animal turned out to be quite blubbery, and the people of Rensselaerswijck boiled off a good quantity of train oil.[12] Even so, the whole river, though flowing strongly at the time, remained oily and covered with grease for up to three weeks afterward. Moreover, as the carcass lay rotting, the stench infected the air to such an extent

9

that it was noticeable nearly two miles to leeward. What may have made this whale ascend the river so far, i.e., forty miles from the nearest salt or brackish water, I cannot say, unless its appetite for the multitude of fish it encountered tempted it and thus drew it from its habitat.

Forty-four miles from the sea the North River divides in two. One branch, through four streams, ascends to the great falls of the Maquas-kil [Mohawk River], known as the Cohoes Falls, of which we shall have more to say presently. The other branch is taken to be a continuation of the main river and remains navigable by a small boat for several miles upstream, and is said by the Indians to run very much farther and to rise in a great lake from which the river of Canada also springs.[13] This is supposed to be the Lake of the Iroquois, which is as big as the Mediterranean Sea, forty miles wide, and stretches beyond the horizon, even when seen from the middle. Its many extensive marshes, reed lands, and swamps are too wide to see across, and great flocks of waterfowl are said to breed there in summer. When the Indians need to cross the lake, the only way they can do so is to set their sights on certain islands in it and go from one island to the next, and to a third or fourth, in as many days' travel. That, however, is as reported by the Indians; some also say that one can travel by small boat from the North River to the river of Canada via the same lake, but that seems to me highly improbable.[14]

The other branch of the North River, as noted above, connects through four streams with the great waterfall of the Maquas-kil. The Indians named it Chahoos [Cohoes], and our people call it the Great Falls. Above it the river widens again to about a hundred paces. The waterfall, at a guess, is between 150 and 200 feet high, and the water pours down as evenly as if it ran down a smooth wall.[15] The edge, wall, and bottom are formed entirely of firm bluestone. Nearby, below the falls, a few rounded rocks rise spectacularly above the water, shaped like hayricks or peat heaps, eight, sixteen, and thirty feet in height and a joy to behold. Were the poets of antiquity in attendance here, they would compose wondrous and pleasing conceits about this location, so conducive to poetic inspiration. Below the falls the water rushes foaming, frisking, and whirling over the stony ground for about the distance of a gunshot and a half, appearing bewildered, then it regains its composure and flows gently on.

Above the falls the river is once again navigable and quite broad; it is called the Maquas-kil. It is broader than the Yssel River in the Netherlands at most points. It flows always in one direction, but being fairly deep, its flow is not rapid or violent. The river passes through all the lands of the Maquas and Scimekas and rises in a lake well over sixty miles distant, remaining navigable throughout.[16] It irrigates great tracts of beautiful country and abounds in fish.

When the Indians travel by water for trading purposes, they always come down this river in watercraft that they know how to make of tree bark.[17] At the falls they must disembark and portage their boats and goods a fair distance overland; else they would be carried by the current over the falls and suffer damage, as happened to an Indian in our time. This Indian, whom I knew well, had sailed down the river in springtime when the flow is strongest, accompanied by his wife and child and about sixty beaver pelts, which he intended to sell to the Dutch. Not taking care to beach his boat in good time, and trusting the stream too little and his own powers too far, the Indian was dragged along before he knew it, and although he naturally did his utmost, when it was too late the rapid flow of water flung him and his little vessel of tree bark downward, together with wife, child, beaver pelts, and other gear he had with him. The wife and child were killed, most of his goods lost or damaged, and his craft broken into many pieces, but he survived. I have often seen him since that time and heard him tell the story.

Of the Fresh River

The Fresh River [Connecticut River], thus named for having an abundance of fresh water, more than any other, is yet another very good location and navigable watercourse. Well-situated fields border it, and it also carries a rather good trade in pelts. But as this river and the adjacent country have been widely invaded and are still held by the English nation, to the great detriment of the honorable West India Company and at a loss of thousands every year, it would only distress us to review this matter, which was very fully treated in the *Remonstrance* of New Netherland. We say no more of it, therefore, and proceed to the East River.

Of the East River

The East River is so named because it extends mostly to the east of the city of New Amsterdam. Some take this river to be only a sound or bay, because it is in some places quite broad and empties at both ends into the ocean, but passing over that subtlety we follow the common judgment and hold it to be a river. River or bay, as one pleases, it is one of the best, commodious, and commendable attributes a country could be desired to have. We shall briefly indicate some of the reasons for this.

The river is shaped by Long Island, which is about forty miles long and can be approached on this river most everywhere through the creeks and inlets into it in both winter and summer with no great hazard. The river also affords convenient and safe passage eastward and westward in all seasons, which is all the more pleasing as the outside or seaward route is not free of danger. Most English vessels heading south, whether to Virginia, the South River, or elsewhere, must pass through the East River, which brings no little trade and prosperity to the city of New Amsterdam, though it also means that the English often have need to frequent our harbors, and we never theirs. This great river, finally, is renowned and deserves to be prized for its multitude of convenient bays, harbors, creeks, inlets, rivers, and other places, in such number on both the island and the inland that we should be unable to find its match in the Netherlands. With this, we feel enough has been said for the time being of this great and famous river of New Netherland.

Of the Various Waters and Their Shapes

Before we leave the subject of water, we add a few general remarks, because to enter into particulars would take too long and exceed our purpose. In New Netherland many fine waterways are to be found—streams, brooks, and creeks that are navigable, wide, and large; also bays, inlets, and settlements, both near the seashore and far inland, as well as many watercourses, streams, and running creeks with many beautiful waterfalls good for all kinds of milling work. Inland there are several standing waters such as big ponds and basins, some as large as lakes, well stocked with fish and fed through veins and streams from marshes and springs and growing to incredible size.

Since little was said of the above in the *Remonstrance*, it would not be out of place to relate the main features of the subject here. As was noted there, apart from the rivers dealt with earlier, there are many and various bays, harbors, and coves that are useful and convenient and could well bear the name of rivers. Inland waters are numerous, some big, others less so, and situated chiefly near the coast south of the North River. Also, great, navigable streams and wide creeks give access to the country most everywhere. There is scope for man-made improvements in many places, and all this can be fully ascertained from the map of New Netherland [p. xxiv]. Several falls,

12

running streams, and brooks also provide sites for watermills of all sorts to serve mankind. Innumerable small creeks and streamlets, like veins in the body, flow conveniently throughout the country. All carry fresh water, except some few on the coast that are occasionally salty or brackish, yet serviceable for watering both wild and domestic animals and draining excess water into the rivers or the sea.

Then there are many fine springs and wells everywhere in the country, even in places where one would not expect to find water, as on mountains, high cliffs, and rocks, where water springs from veins and seeps down. Some springs are greatly prized because they become very clear and amazingly pure streams, other than in thickets where they catch no sun or are frequented by game or soiled by weeds, falling leaves, and rotting vegetation. Many also have this property, that in the bitter cold of winter they give off vapor and do not freeze, and quickly thaw anything placed in them; yet in the hottest time of the summer the water is so cold, even if exposed all day to direct sunlight, that one cannot bear to hold his hand in it. That quality renders the water very pleasant and fit for use by man and beast, for it can be taken without any danger. Though fatigued and heated, a person taking this water suffers no ill effects, no matter how hot the weather may be. Many drink this water, yet I have never heard from hunters, woodsmen, or even Indians that anyone contracted pleurisy or similar ailments from it.

The Indians sometimes make report of other sources of water quite different in taste from the usual and having special powers and qualities that are beneficial in the treatment of various complaints and diseases. Whether this is exactly as the Indians tell us, I am not sure, but it may be, seeing that the country abounds in minerals and metals, and that veins of water seeping through them could partake of and in some measure retain their properties.[18]

It is a great advantage and virtue of the land in New Neth-erland that one is not plagued by severe flooding or inunda-tions, for near the seashore, or as far as salt or brackish water comes up, there is no abnormal flood tide. The water level rises and subsides with the regular tides by five or six feet. In places that are to a greater or lesser degree exposed to winds and cur-rents, the tides are very strong, though not violent. At spring tide, when the wind comes in from the sea, the water may ascend a foot or two higher than normal, but that happens but seldom, so that few are inconvenienced by it. Farther inland, however, as in the colony of Rensselaerswijck, Catskill, Eso-pus, and thereabouts, at the headwaters where the rivers are entirely fresh, low-lying land may be flooded once or twice a year when the wind blows counter to the current, but to those who prepare and provide for it this causes no damage. Some-times a stand of corn here and there is washed away, though the silt left behind as good as manures the land. Nor does the water remain standing for long; as quickly as it rises, it ebbs away again in two or three days.

Of the Formation and Soil of the Land

Having spoken of the waters, we now proceed to the land, its produce and surface, and begin with its formation, which is as follows. Along and near the coast the land is not very high, with several hills and mounds, and for the most part sandy or shingly. It is always mixed with clay, however, which enriches it so that it produces naturally a variety of trees and bushes, fruits, and wild herbs. Heaths or similar arid and barren lands are not found there at all. The entire country has a generally undulating surface with high hills in some places and, occasionally, big and prominent mountains, as in the so-called highlands in particular. This is an area of high mountain ranges of some three miles wide, which run like a crescent through the country, sloping down at some points and then rising and continuing again.[19] Yet there are also so many beautiful flats with meadows and pastures of great length and breadth, both in the river and along the water's edge.[20] As everywhere else in the country, most hills are not steep but rise gently so that one sometimes finds oneself on very high ground overlooking plains, valleys, and tall trees before one is aware of having ascended. Such land affords fine views for the enjoyment of painters and hunters, for it has many pleasing prospects, shadows, hills, watercourses, and valleys, and, for the hunter in particular, deer and other wildlife feeding on the hillsides or in the valleys.

14 The soil normally consists of black earth mixed with clay down to about a foot or a foot and a half, and sometimes a bit more or less—but this is the way it commonly occurs. Below that there is mostly off-white, reddish, or yellow clay with perhaps some gravel, and here and there a layer of rocks large or small and variously tinted. Some hills consist purely of clay and fuller's earth, but sand hills I have not seen other than along the beach as thrown up by the sea. Then there are rocky hills formed of stones and judged by experts to be minerals or of mineral content. Part of the mountainous area is arable, the rest clad with forest. Some hills are of pure clay and others of earth and stones, and a few, mostly in the highlands, consist of nothing but rocks in various colors and shapes, yet are covered with trees growing everywhere in clefts and crevices. Amid the mountains and hills throughout the country, and by the rivers and shores, lie great and wide plains measuring hundreds, even thousands of *morgens*, which are very suitable for establishing villages, settlements, farms, and plantations.[21]

There are also wetlands and marshes—salt, fresh, or brackish—some so big that one cannot see across them. They can be used for pasture or haymaking only, because they tend to flood at spring tide if situated near the coast. They resemble the mud flats and river meadows of the Netherlands and could be drained with the aid of levees and plowed. Marshlands are also found inland, far from the rivers, and they are always fresh and good for haymaking, provided they are not too clumpy or too wet. These defects can be overcome with little trouble if one makes the effort by breaking up the clods when frozen in winter and drawing off the water in spring at a suitable opportunity. There would be many more freshwater marshes but for the land's natural condition favoring the growth of trees and the wide dispersal of seed by birds and wind, so that the dampest and wettest areas also become wooded. These are known as thickets and are so densely overgrown with trees and brushwood of every kind, mostly of small size in between the bigger specimens, that it is a marvel to behold. Still, when this land is cleared and brought under the plow, it is fertile beyond compare.

So much, then, is too briefly noted here and in what follows regarding the formation of the land. I pray the indulgent reader to deduce from the above how fertile this land is and form his own judgment; as to myself, I confess to being unable to depict it or show it in writing, since in my view the eye alone, more so than the ear, is capable of comprehending it.

Of Wood and Vegetation

New Netherland is fortunate in being highly productive also of fine species of trees in such measure that they cover almost the whole country and, in a manner of speaking, are too plentiful and in the way. Yet this comes in useful for building ships and houses as well as for fencing farmland. Oak trees may grow to a height of fifty, sixty, or seventy feet, are free of irksome knots, heavy, and sometimes up to two fathoms around. They come in several varieties, such as smooth bark, rough bark, pale gray bark, and black bark. The wood is fully as good and durable, if properly worked, as that of the Rhine or the Weser regions; thus I was informed by several experts and local woodsmen who had viewed samples of both.

Hickory grows quite as tall but not as heavy, and it may well be believed that it could in time be put to various uses, being very straight, tough, smooth, and hard. Now we do little more with it than make cogs and shafts for mills, also threshing flails and harrows for tillage, because it is so tough. Further, we use it as firewood, for which it is very good, in contradiction to the old adage that the man who can improve on oak for firewood is yet to appear. Hickory far surpasses oak in heat as well as lasting quality. Thanks to its oily sap it always burns whether green or wet, even if freshly taken out of water and saturated with it, while its hard consistency renders it especially long lasting in the fire. Therefore one may honestly say that no peat or other combustible common in this country can equal it, and when dry it holds the fire and sparkles away like a fuse. Some women also praise its charcoal as used in stoves and say it works better than peat, for it lasts well and does not get buried in ashes. Hickory occurs all over New Netherland in such abundance and quantity that there will be no shortage of it for a hundred years to come, even if the population were to grow appreciably. There is also enough oak and ash to supplement the hickory wood.

Apart from that, the soil favors the growth of big trees in just a few years, as I can frankly state and conclude from a particular event I experienced in that country. Once when I was discussing various matters with some *wilden* (as we call those natives not born of Christian parents) one of them said to me, while we were standing near a young forest, "I see that you are having that land made ready for use; you will do well, it is very good land and bears grain in great quantity; I know that, because only twenty-five or twenty-six years ago we planted grain there, and now it has reverted to forest."[22] I asked him earnestly if that was truly so, and he assured me it was, as several other Indians present also testified. Now to get to the point. This was a stand of hickory and mostly oak where several trees measured a fathom around, many half that and so on, but so closely spaced that only with the greatest difficulty could one have passed through it on horseback. That made it all the easier for me to accept and believe that this forest was quite young, because I have often observed while living there that young forests are particularly dense, and the very young ones hardly penetrable, but accordingly, as the forest ages and the trees grow bigger, many others, being stifled and obstructed, lag behind and are eliminated.

The Indians are in the habit—and we Christians have also adopted it—once a year in the fall to burn the woods, plains, and those marshlands that are not too wet as soon as the leaves have dropped and the herbage has withered. Portions that were missed, as may happen, get their turn later in the months of March or April. This is known among our people as well as the Indians there as bush burning and is practiced for several reasons, some of which we shall briefly note. For one, it facilitates hunting, because the dry weeds and fallen leaves not only hinder the hunter's progress, but the crackling invariably betrays him and the game spot him first. Second, it serves to thin out the forest as the fire smothers and kills much new undergrowth. Third, it clears the forest of old dead-wood consisting of branches and fallen trees; and fourth, it increases the game and assists the hunter since it restricts the animals' movements and also enables them to be tracked in the burned areas.

Bush burning is an extraordinary and spectacular event. Seen from a distance it would seem that not only the leaves, weeds, and deadwood are being consumed, but that all the trees and the whole of the surrounding forest are falling prey to the flames. Fall being a dry season over there, the fire burns so fiercely and spreads so fast that it is terrifying to watch. When the fire rages near houses, homesteads, and wooden fencing, one has to be careful lest he suffer damage, as happened at first before people watched out for it, when several houses burned down. Green trees are not at risk, however; the outer bark is charred for a foot or two from the ground, but it does not kill them. In very dense stands of pine trees that are old and resinous, it happens that the fire sweeps upward, because dying trees have fallen against and across each other or remained halfway standing and dried out. In those trees the fire settles and spreads upward along them, and when it reaches the gluey, resinous branches and knots, it begins to blaze fiercely and flies from tree to tree, so that sometimes a good part of the top only is burned away, and the bottom remains standing. Many trees are thus destroyed, but it never happens that all the bush burns down. I have seen many instances of it in the colony of Rensselaerswijck, which has much pinewood.[23] Such a fire is a spectacular sight when one sails on the rivers at night while the forest is ablaze on both banks. Fire and flames are seen everywhere and on all sides. Much of the blaze is driven on by the wind and follows what it feeds on, but in many spots dry wood and dead trees keep on burning; it is a delightful scene to look on from afar.

It is clear, then, that New Netherland has such an abundance of wood that it will never be wanting, and that those people such as are often encountered are unnecessarily worried, who fear that wood may come to be in short supply and therefore judge that one ought not to make such liberal use of it. This is so far from the truth that to country folk engaged in farming and planting, nothing appears more useful or needful than to fell the woods around them, so that they often burn big piles of wood on the land just to be rid of it, because it is in the way.

The country also has very serviceable pinewood and, as we

were told by Norwegians living there, local timber of white pine, spruce, and white cedar is as good as it is in Norway. Pines are not so common near the sea and saltwater shores, some places excepted, but far inland and at the upper reaches of the rivers pine trees abound, whole forests of them, and big enough for ships' masts and all kinds of spars.

Chestnut trees are like those in the Netherlands, but they grow dispersed in the forests. They would be more plentiful than they are if the Indians did not damage so many of them for the sake of the smooth and unbroken bark, which comes off easily and which they use in great quantity for roofing their houses. Also, when the Indians, and even the Dutch, go out gathering chestnuts, they are in the habit of chopping down the trees at knee height or cutting off all the branches, and that rather reduces their number.[24]

Beeches come in several varieties, but they bear few nuts. One variety, the water beech, grows to a very great size, taller and heavier than any tree normally grows in this country. Its bark is attractive when looked at from below, particularly on the older trees. Not only has the wood by then become markedly white, but the bark takes on the appearance of white satin. The tree keeps its leaves longer than any other tree in the woods; the leaves are very big and thick and from beneath outward colored ash gray, making it that much more pleasant and decorative for planting near homes. Just as it is with the lindens of this country, we cannot suggest a local equivalent nor give the tree another name for identifying it.[25]

There are also hornbeams, some growing into big trees; junipers, whose wood resembles cedar; and tulip trees, of which the Indians make their boats because they are so big.[26] Our people often use this wood for ceiling and floorboards, because it is very white and free of knots and has a shine. Then there is ash of two varieties, linden, birch, elm, poplar, aspen, alder, willow, various thorn trees, sassafras, persimmon, mulberry, holly, crab, and several others, big and small, whose names are unknown to us but which could be used for various purposes.[27] Only some of those trees bear fruit.

There are oak trees of different kinds that bear acorns usually every other year, resembling chestnuts; various nut trees, the nuts being about the same size as those at home; persimmon, but differing somewhat from ours and not as good; the mulberries are better than ours, since they ripen in early summer and are also much harder and sweeter; several varieties of plums; small wild cherries; juniper berries; various small apples; many hazelnuts; black currants; gooseberries, prickly pears; and strawberries all over the country, as good as those at home, which normally ripen by the middle of May and last until July; blueberries; cranberries; raspberries; blackberries; mushrooms; etc.[28] Also artichokes, growing underground; earth chestnuts; groundnuts; wild onions; leeks, which are like our own; and several other roots and fruits that the Indians know how to prepare and eat in time of need.[29] The Dutch do not value them, however, because all sorts of garden vegetables imported from here thrive and grow so well there. The country also has many button-shaped fruits like Spanish capers, which could be trained up.

Of the Fruit Trees Brought Over from the Netherlands

Dutch horticulturists, noting the opportunities existing in New Netherland, have ventured to carry across and plant various apple and pear trees that thrive there. The trees will also grow from seed, and I have seen specimens that by the sixth year bore delicious fruit without having been grafted. If stocks or cuttings are not available, grafting also works well on a trunk cut off close to the ground, so that in time the graft itself makes roots; otherwise the fruit may be rather stony. In general, though, grafting is not as necessary as it is here, for most of the fruit is good without it, whereas in this country the tree would bear tart and tough fruit or none at all. The English brought over the first quinces; our people later on sent over quince slips and stocks, and these grow and bear well. Orchard cherries also grow there and bear large and good fruit; Spanish cherries, sweet cherries, and morellos occur in several varieties, as in this country, but the crop is more certain, because no harm to the blossoms from inclement spring weather need be feared.

The cherry tree thrives remarkably well; for instance, it often happens in New Netherland that when the pit is put into the ground, it sprouts the same year and grows so quickly that the tree bears fruit in the fourth year. The trees carry such a weight of fruit that sometimes they crack or the branches break off. The peaches are tasty as well; there are also nectarines, brought over by our people, besides apricots, many varieties of the best plums, almonds, persimmons, cornel cherries, figs, several kinds of red currants, Dutch gooseberries, licorice, and clove trees. Olives could no doubt be cultivated successfully, but they have not yet been introduced. Though grape vines occur naturally, the best cuttings obtained locally and from Germany have been sent across to allow vintners to experiment with them and propagate the best. In short, many kinds of fruit trees and plant varieties that grow in this country are now already plentiful in New Netherland or are being imported by fanciers. Some thrive also much more naturally than they do here, mainly those requiring warm weather.

Of the Vineyards

It is unbelievable in what profusion grapevines grow wild in New Netherland; no region or corner of the country is without them.[30] They grow on the level and open fields, in the natural forests under the trees, on the banks of rivers, creeks, and streams, on the hillsides, and on the foothills of mountains. Some vines grow up trees, spread over coppices, shrubs, and brushwood, or through the grass on the ground, so that when on horseback or on foot one becomes entangled in them; it often takes much effort and time to get free again. Vines running up trees usually do not bear much fruit, but in some years practically all produce in abundance, and it is truly a delight and natural wonder to see such choice and lovely fruit growing rank and wild all over. Many regard it as without equal. When the vines are in bloom, a delightful scent pervades the open country, making it a joy to stroll or pass through it.

It is sad but true that the grapes rarely ripen in season, if at all, when vines climb up tree trunks or hide beneath coppices and brushwood, are not pruned, looked after, or cultivated at all, and the sun never touches the root stock. The reason given is that they cannot spread to the outermost twigs of the trees, are overshadowed by the branches and leaves, and never enjoy the full sun. Therefore, the grapes are tarter, stonier, and pulpier than they otherwise might be. The proof is that if any vines happen to have spread up a dead tree and thus enjoy the warmth of the sun unobstructed by foliage, the grapes are much sweeter and ripen earlier; and there are quite a few trees in the forest that have withered because the Indians removed the bark for use in building their houses and boats. The same is true of vines that grow on the banks of creeks and brooks having a southern exposure, where they catch the sun, as I and those around me have often found to be so. In such a spot, in mid-August, I have not only seen ripe grapes but also picked and eaten them, though normally they do not ripen quite so early.

One must also bear in mind that the roots of the wine stocks are not treated in any way, never trimmed, or watered, or manured—which in our view would hasten fruition if it were done. By bringing those means and human industry to bear on such willing forces of nature, it cannot be doubted that, in general, wines as good as from any quarter of Germany or France will be the result. Evidence of this can be seen on the South River, for there the Swedish residents placed very old rootstock in the soil, which they call planting suckers, and they obtain and enjoy many fine, delightful wines from it, year after year.

The grape and its juice are not all of one kind or color. There are grapes with a bluish skin, some lighter than others, a few are reddish, others quite white like muscatels, so in general, they come in four colors. The grapes and the bunches vary in size; the white and the red are about as big as the best Netherlands muscatels, while the blue may be big or small. The big grapes tend to be pulpy and are therefore commonly known as port grapes, but the experts consider that proper cultivation will remove that defect. The juice is as elsewhere, either clear white or ruddy, in some cases red like French wine. The last, to my knowledge, comes only from the big blue grapes. Then there is juice of such a deep red color and so viscous that it resembles dragon's blood more than wine. One wine glass of it can tint a jug of water bright red as though it were ordinary red wine.

Our Dutch people, not hailing from wine-growing country, have never taken much trouble over it, haphazardly planting a grapevine or two but never properly looking after it. At times they have pressed a quantity of grapes, but no one with the right understanding or knowledge was ever involved with it, so that nothing very worthwhile resulted. Yet I have more than once drunk a fairly good and palatable wine, and we observed that the fault lay with us and not with the vineyard.

A year or two ago, however, some interested persons, previously apprised of the situation, forwarded several shoots and plants there. Also, a German born near Heidelberg was expressly sent over with instructions to provide himself with

21

Of the Vineyards | 27

Vitis australis
V. labrusca
V. riparia

Summer gr | mich
Fox gr.
Frost gr. | Tucker
Riverbank gr |

anything still lacking and with skilled workmen. Accordingly, wine growing has begun to be undertaken in earnest, so that there are now several formal wine estates and wine hills. The good Lord has blessed these endeavors and made them bear fruit, so I am informed. Vineyards are now set to increase from year to year, for everyone takes it up and the one learns from the other. Seeing that the population of New Netherland is growing strongly now, an abundance of wine may be expected in a few short years.

Of Vegetables Generally

The vegetables in New Netherland are many and varied, some known of old among the Indians, others brought over from other parts, though mostly from the Netherlands. We shall say something of vegetables in general, but fanciers would be able to relate many more attractive attributes of them, since we, having had other needful things to do, have never gone into this subject.

The local vegetables comprise several varieties of lettuce, cabbages, parsnips, yellow and red carrots, beets, endives, chicory, fennel, sorrel, dill, spinach, radishes, horseradishes, parsley, chervil, onions, chives, and whatever else is normally found in a cabbage or kitchen garden. The herb garden is also fairly well supplied with rosemary, lavender, hyssop, thyme, sage, marjoram, balm, garlic, wormwood, toadflax, leek, and clary; also burnet, dragon's blood, cinquefoil, tarragon, etc., besides laurel, artichokes, and asparagus, and various other items I do not know or have not noticed.[31] Naturalists report that the vegetables there are drier and hence more vigorous than in this country. I have also observed that they are less cared for and cultivated and yet grow equally well.

Pumpkins grow with little or no cultivating. They are so sweet and dry that for the purpose of preparing them water and vinegar are added before stewing them in the same way as apples. While here they are regarded as an insipid, poor, and despised food, over there they turn out so well that our people relish them. I have been told that when properly prepared, as apples are here, they are not inferior to apples or differ only slightly, and when baked in an oven they are considered even better than apples. The English, who are fond of tasty food, like pumpkins very much and use them also in pies, and know how to make a beverage from them. I am not sure whether all kinds of pumpkins and gourds occurring anywhere are also to be found there, but the Spanish are the best of all.

22

The Indians also have their own kind of pumpkin, called by the Dutch *Quaesiens* or *Cascoeten*, which name they borrowed from the Indians, because that kind was previously unknown to us.[32] It is a pleasing fruit, both to the eye for its many beautiful colors and to the palate for its good taste. Housemaids appreciate them as they are easy to prepare. The fruit becomes available early in summer, for if the seeds are planted in mid-April, it is fit for eating by the beginning of June. One need not wait for the squashes to ripen before eating them; when they reach a certain size, they are picked and straightaway put on the fire without further preparation. After the first picking they should be gathered every three or four days. It is incredible how many squashes grow on one plant in a year, if picked regularly. The shoots run along the ground for a short distance of a yard or two; they will also grow in newly broken woodland, provided it is cleared a little and weeds are kept out. The Indians make much use of this fruit, and some Netherlanders consider it quite good, but others pay little attention to it. It is a fruit that is easy to grow, prepare, and digest, and is reasonably tasty and nourishing.

Melons also grow easily in New Netherland without tilling and manuring of the land being necessary. Pruning these plants is hardly known there, nor [is] propagating them painstakingly under glass, as is done here. Were they to receive the attentive care that cucumbers do here, the results would be highly satisfactory. Growers plant melons even when they no longer expect the fruit to ripen, and if by mischance some plants die off, new seed is put into the ground. Melons also grow well in newly broken woodland if kept free of brushwood. Once planted, this fruit, known locally as Spanish bacon, grows very luxuriantly and big. Those who from curiosity have weighed them found some to be seventeen pounds in weight. Owing to the warm climate the melons over there are more delicious and pleasant to eat and will not disagree with anyone however many he eats, provided they are fully ripe.

The country also produces citrullines, or watermelons, a fruit not grown here but occasionally imported from Portugal and otherwise known only to those who have traveled in warmer climes like New Netherland.[33] This vegetable grows and proliferates more abundantly than the melon, so much so that some people plant it in order effectively to clear the land and subdue natural woodland for turning into arable fields. The juice is delicious and rather like apricot juice. People there will eat as many as six watermelons against one melon, even when they can have as many of both as they wish. Watermelons normally grow as big as a man's head. I have seen some the size of the stoutest Leiden cabbages, except that they have more of an oblong shape. Inside they are white or red; the red have red pits, and the white black pits. When they are to be eaten, the rind is cut off to about a finger thick. All the rest is very good to eat—a light-textured pulp like a wet sponge in which the pits are embedded. When really ripe and sound, it melts away to a juice as soon as it enters the mouth, and nothing remains to spit out but the pits. Women and children love watermelons; they are also very refreshing and often served as a beverage. I have heard from the English that they make a drink out of watermelons, which is a match for Spanish wine, though not so heady; also, that it does have the defect of easily turning sour, and that the vinegar produced from it lasts well and is so good that it is much used.

Cucumbers are abundant. Calabashes are also grown there; this is a fruit similar to a long-necked pumpkin but containing very little pulp. They are sought chiefly for their shells, which, being hard and strong, have many uses, such as holding seeds, spices, and similar things. The calabash is the usual water pail of the Indians, and I have seen them so big that they could hold more than a *skipple*.[34] Turnips are as good and firm as any sand turnip in this country can be. Then there are peas and various sorts of beans. The peas we shall discuss under field crops.

Beans come in great variety, but neither the broad beans, which the farmers here also call *tessen* or house beans, nor the horse beans, will bear fruit; the leaf growth is lush and profuse enough, and a plant may produce ten or twelve shoots, yet bear little or nothing.[35] Green beans, introduced there by our people, grow luxuriantly, bear extremely well, and are much cultivated. Before our arrival the Indians already had beans of various kinds and colors but rather too pulpy for eating green or for pickling, except the blue variety, which has no such fault. Their white beans, more so than the Dutch kind, tend to cause flatulence but are otherwise good food.[36] The Indians are particularly fond of these beans and have an interesting way of planting them—which the Netherlanders have meanwhile copied: When the Turkish wheat, as corn is known there, is half a foot above the ground, they plant the beans in between and let them grow up together. The corn being ahead, its coarse stalks serve as bean poles along which the beans run up, and thus two crops are raised at the same time.

Of the Flowers

The flowers taken there by the Hollanders include white and red roses of various types, also peonies and hollyhocks. There was none of the following before then: sweetbriers, various carnations, stocks, many fine tulips, snake's head, white lilies, the mottled lily, anemones, daffodils, violets, marigolds, snowdrops, etc.[37] Clove trees were also taken there. Indigenous to the country are several other trees bearing pretty flowers, unknown here. The country also has certain flowers of its own, namely, sunflowers, red and yellow lilies, Turk's cap lilies, salsifies, white, red, and yellow daisies—a sweet little flower —and many bell-shaped flowers, etc., to which I have paid no particular attention, but fanciers could collect quite a few and make them widely known.

Of the Medicinal Herbs and Indigo

That there are various healing herbs and medicinal plants in New Netherland cannot be doubted. A certain surgeon once laid out a fine garden and, as he was a botanist as well, planted many medicinal species he had found growing wild, but with his departure this came to an end. I suppose that, sickness being so infrequent there, the subject is receiving correspondingly little attention. The medicinal plants now known there comprise in the main: *Capilli veneris, Scholopentria, Angelica, Polupodium, Verbascum album, Calteus sacerdotis, Atriplex hortense* and *marine, Chortium, Turrites, Calamus aromaticus, Sassafrax, Rois virginianum, Ranunculas, Plantago, Burso pastoris, Malva, Origaenum, Gheranicum, Althea, Cinoroton psuydo, Daphine, Viola, Ireas, Indigo silvestris, Sigilum salamonis, Sanguis dracoum, Consolidae, Mille folium, Noli metanghere, Cardo benedictus, Agrunonium, Serpentanae,* coriander, curly docks, wild leeks, Spanish fig, *Elaetine, Camperfoelie, Petum*—male and female—and a variety of ferns.[38] Moreover, the country is full of all kinds of plants and trees, so that there are undoubtedly numerous good specifics. Experts could do much in that direction, all the more so, we believe, since the Indians are able to heal frightful open wounds and ugly old sores with mere roots, bulbs, and leaves. We could cite many examples of this but for the sake of brevity pass it by.

Indigo silvestris grows naturally in that country without needing any cultivation or human aid.[39] If knowledgeable persons were to go in for it, much profit could no doubt be derived from it. Proof of this was seen in the colony of Rensselaerswijck; Mr. Kiliaen van Rensselaer, who lived and died a great supporter and admirer of New Netherland, sent seed over, but it was sown late and in an unsuitable site where no grass would grow. That was on Beeren Island, which consists of rock with less than a foot of soil on top, so that the seed sprouted well but the plants turned yellow and withered in the dry summer.[40] Still, one can see that it would have been a success if it had been correctly done. Afterward, one Augustijn Heermans, likewise a notable champion of New Netherland, once again undertook the sowing of indigo near the city of New Amsterdam.[41] It succeeded and produced a good yield. Samples sent home were found to be good, and better than the ordinary sort.

The planting of madder root has never been attempted here, though it could no doubt be done, for the soil in many places is rich and heavy enough. Mr. Minuit writes that he made a trial of sowing canary seed and that it was successful and yielded well, but as the settlement was then in its early stages, he adds, the people were reluctant to spend their time on such things and rather made sure they had the essential foodstuffs.[42] Of those there are now, praise the Lord, more than enough and reasonably cheap, so that food and drink are beginning to be supplied to other countries in the vicinity, such as Virginia, the West Indies, and the Caribbean Islands. This is expected to increase year by year and in time to become good business, particularly if the trade with Netherlands Brazil were to be added.[43]

Of Agriculture and Field Crops

Farming in New Netherland is not as laborious and difficult as it is in this country, primarily because fencing and enclosing are not so costly, for instead of our ditches and canals, people there put up posts, pickets, or rails. Where new farmland is being prepared, wood is usually to be found on the site at the cost of labor only. Farm labor is reasonably available to those who have their own workers; without help not much can be achieved. Land with few trees, or fairly well cleared and plowed twice, is considered quite ready for sowing all winter crops. For summer crops one plowing is enough, and if a winter crop of rye or wheat is to be sown next, the stubble is plowed under and the seed is sown right in, and in good years will grow well.

I can say that in the nine years or so I lived in that country, I never saw the land being fertilized; it is certainly seldom done. Soil quality is maintained more often by leaving land fallow, both because it gets overgrown with weeds and scrub and because it needs resting. People whom I regard as quite competent sow their land with peas when it becomes weedy and they reckon it needs to be rested, because this is said to make the soil soft, rich, and clean.[44] Much of the land is too fertile for peas, however, and if sown there the plants grow so rank that they soon fall over and rot on the ground. Such land must first be broken in by planting wheat and barley before it can take peas. Even so, it has often been experienced that the winter grain crop also grew too luxuriant, so that the yield of wheat or rye was not nearly as great as it might have been. The most common variety of peas are the big gray ones known as old crones, having blue and white and also big white pods. They are sown mostly in the vegetable garden rather than the fields.

It is worth telling, and I cannot omit doing so at this point, that in that country ripe peas normally can be harvested twice a year from the same land if good care is taken. It has been done several times in this manner: One sows peas in late March or early April, depending on the season, and they ripen early in July, when they are harvested. The land is plowed once again and is immediately sown with the same seed it has produced. Thus one has ripe peas again in September or early October, when the weather often remains fine and summery for quite some time. The same could be done with buckwheat, as I have been told by reliable persons who said they had tried it, but as buckwheat suffers much damage from finches and other birds, and wheat and rye are abundant, it is not much cultivated, the more so as corn takes the place of it everywhere.

Turkish wheat, or corn as it is called there, and which many believe to be the same as the roasted corn that Jesse, David's father, ordered him to take to his brothers in the encampment, is a very versatile grain.[45] It has many uses both for planting and otherwise and will grow in any soil, even the poorest and stoniest, however farmed out and weedy it may be. Corn is also good for turning woodland into farmland, for once the bushes and trees on the land have been chopped down and burned, one digs holes with broad pickaxes six feet apart and drops half a dozen kernels in each. Then one can stick in Turkish beans as well, if so desired, as mentioned earlier. While it is growing, two weedings are enough. Nor is the weeding very hard work, for the soil is not turned but merely cleared of weeds on top with a broad mattock. The first time, the weeds are piled up between the rows; the second time is easier as only the new growth is killed and the first lot is raked into small heaps around the cornstalks. Meanwhile the corn grows high and tall and smothers all the undergrowth and stumps and scrub beneath it, so that nothing remains alive. Pumpkins alone will grow among the corn, their shoots running everywhere between and through the rows.

When the land has been tilled in that way for one summer, it is ready for various uses, either to plant corn again, which will then grow better and with much less effort than the first time, or to plant tobacco or to bring it under the plow. Plowing will now be easier, as the roots will have been choked, smothered, and partly decayed, and will come up out of the ground and break into pieces. One can also, after the corn has been harvested, sow winter grain without plowing. In that case the cornstalks are pulled up and burned, the [corn] hills raked apart, the wheat sown and lightly harrowed under, and a good wheat crop will result. I have known rye to be sown as related above, which yet grew so tall that a man of normal stature could tie it together above his head, and in addition, so heavy that it yielded seven or eight bushels Amsterdam measure per haycock, the latter being equal to 108 sheaves or half a cartload.[46] The Reverend Johannis Megapolensis Junior, former minister to the colony of Rensselaerswijck, wrote about the subject in a letter to his friends, later issued by them in print contrary to his intention, as I have learned from him personally.[47] He can be believed, being a man of great learning, and he could have put the matter even more strongly. He relates inter alia that a certain husbandman told him he had reaped wheat eleven times in eleven successive years on one and the same field.[48] To many people this is a strong claim and they can hardly credit it, yet it is true. Those who have lived over there can vouch for it, and more. From the beginning until the eleventh crop that land had not been plowed more than twelve times, that is, twice at first, and from then on the stubble was plowed under and the land seeded eleven times in all. I owned adjacent land and have seen the eleventh crop: it was fairly good. The name of the man to whom it happened was Brandt Pelen, who hailed from the bishopric of Utrecht and at the time was *schepen* in the colony of Rensselaerswijck.[49] Admittedly this seems rather strange at first sight, but over there it is no miracle; there are many thousands of *morgens* as good and as fertile as the land spoken of here. It happened, too, in the time when I resided in that country, that a certain honorable man by the name of Jan Evertsz Bout, a commissioner of their excellencies [the States General] to the commonalty of New Netherland, wagered for a sum of money that his stand of barley of seven *morgens* in extent, if I remember rightly, was so fine and tall that there were no plants among them that a man could not easily tie together above his head.[50] Upon which the parties went to inspect the farm and found the stalks to be on average between six and seven feet tall and only a very few to be shorter. I have also been told as the truth that barley has often yielded eleven bushels Amsterdam measure per haycock, though that is not usual. Therefore all expert and interested persons judge that New Netherland is as fertile and fit for growing all kinds of grain as any part of the world thus far known to or possessed by Netherlanders. Among the field crops tobacco is also to be included, since it is also grown on farmland and is also good for breaking in and preparing the soil in the same way and at least as well as corn is. Tobacco returns fully as much profit when it is looked after and grows well and luxuriantly there, so that not only I, but hundreds with me, have seen many leaves that we estimated at up to five quarters [of an ell] in length.[51] The tobacco there is lovely and fragrant, differs little in flavor from Varinas, and though the latter is better, the difference is more in the price than the quality.[52] It may well be the next best to Varinas and by many is considered superior to Virginian tobacco. Many expect, and it is indeed likely, that as the population multiplies there and more tobacco is planted, the product will gain in renown and prominence, and that the defect in flavor, attributed by some solely to impurity of the soil as a result of hasty cultivation, will be entirely removed or much diminished.

Barley does well over there but is not yet in demand. Cumin, canary seed, and the like have been tried, and Commander Minuit testifies that they thrive extremely well, but such things are not at present so essential as to be pursued. Flax and hemp grown there are quite good, though not much cultivated because the womenfolk do little or no spinning, and the Indians have their own supplies of hemp in the woods, sufficient for their needs, of which they make strong ropes and nets for their own use. Thus little flax or hemp is grown there, but from the amount that is grown, one can tell that the quality is good and serviceable.

Of the Minerals and the Kinds of Earth and Stone

Observers of New Netherland's mild climate and its appearance and formation, most of it being fairly high, free of flooding and surges, and in many places mountainous and hilly, will readily believe and notice that it contains minerals. Yet the Netherlanders have never spent much effort and money on investigating or prospecting, not from negligence as some think, but, in our opinion, for good reasons. It has long been the commonly held view in that country that there must surely be many precious and excellent minerals—gold as well as other precious metals. But then that would have to be investigated in a different way, and the common people do not readily do that, nor does the government seem to be so inclined. On the other hand, people forget that the Netherlanders there were few in number and that minerals, if better and more precious than iron, attract everyone's attention, including that of envious suitors who, in due course, might well have slammed the door in our face and enjoyed the maiden's favors. Leaving that aside, however, we shall report some particulars of what happened both over there and in this country, for the information of interested persons, so that there may be no doubt that minerals are to be found there as has been undeniably proved by tests that were made. In the time of Director Willem Kieft, and by his honor's order, several tests for gold as well as quicksilver were performed in his presence.[53] It is still fresh in my memory that I was present and witnessed some of them, and that the samples were found to be good and of a high grade. Attempts were made from time to time to send samples over to the fatherland, but that was never successful. In 1645 a mine was discovered by chance in the Raritans, which was considered to be better and more valuable than any previously known.[54] It was much talked about among the people in those days, and therefore, we think it worthwhile for the benefit of those interested [in minerals] to tell the whole story briefly and truthfully. In the year 1645 negotiations were in progress between the governing officials of the colony of Rensselaerswijck and the Maquas [Mohawk] Indians—then and now the strongest and most feared nation in the country—in order to bring to a peaceful conclusion the disaffection and wars between Director Willem Kieft, on the one hand, and the neighboring Indian nation, on the other.[55] The party from Rensselaerswijck had brought with them as interpreter a certain Indian named Agheroense, who was accustomed to being among Christians and also understood very well all the major Indian languages in use among the parties.[56] Now the Indians are in the habit of decorating their faces, using paints in various conspicuous colors, the brighter and shinier the better they like it. It happened one morning that this Indian, who had spent the night in the director's house, came downstairs, sat down, and in my and the director's presence—the latter being at that time also in the Rensselaerswijck delegation to the peace talks—began applying coloring to his face. Observing this, the director requested that I ask him for the material he was putting on, and he handed it to me and I to the director. After the director had inspected it at length, he judged from its heaviness and greasy shine that it was some precious mineral. The Indian was compensated for the material so that it might be examined for what was in it. It was put in a crucible and treated as best one could according to directions from one Johannes La Montagne, doctor of medicine and councilor in New Netherland, a wise man who also had some knowledge of such matters.[57] To be brief, when the material was judged to have been on the fire long enough, it was taken off, and it yielded two nuggets of gold worth about three guilders for the two. The test was kept quiet at first, and after peace had been made and concluded, some persons with a company official were dispatched to the mountain, which the Indian had indicated perfectly. They returned with a good bucketful of earth and rock they had dug up where they thought best, not having any special knowledge. Of this material a few more trials were made, all yielding the same outcome as the first, so that the question was regarded as settled. The director agreed to send most of the best remaining material to the fatherland with a person by the name of Arent Corsen via New Haven, from where a ship would be sailing to England about Christmas time, but as fate would have it this came to naught, since it has never been ascertained where the ship ended up; it is supposed to have been lost at sea.[58] When Director Willem Kieft left for the fatherland in 1647, he also had some of those and other specimens with him for testing, but owing to the shipwreck of the *Princes* with the director on board, the specimens were also lost.[59] I have now been informed by one Cornelis van Tienhoven, secretary of New Netherland, who is currently here in Holland, that he has had tests performed here on the same material, all of which were successful so that few doubt its quality.[60] I have thought it right to record that instance here; many more like it could be adduced, but it would be tedious to elaborate each one in detail. Nonetheless, one finds in that country all sorts of alluvial sediments and indications of mineral deposits, chiefly of iron. The New Englanders already manufacture and cast their own cannon, sheet iron, pots, bullets, etc., of the ore in their territory. By now there are persons in New Netherland who are acquainted with that industry and who declare that New Netherland has much better and richer ore-bearing mountains than New England has, but in our humble view it would not be advisable to do anything more about it or to continue exploring until such areas are more fully settled. Some mountains consist solely of fuller's earth, and several of other kinds of fine earth or clay, some white, others red, yellow, blue, gray, and black, all very greasy and sticky, and probably suitable for making such articles as dishes, pots, platters, and tobacco pipes. Good earth for brick and tile making is also found, as I know from experience. It is a pity, therefore, that not more people in those trades move there, because they could undoubtedly do good business and the country would also benefit. Then there is mountain crystal, glass such as comes from Moscovy, and also large amounts of serpentine stone of a brighter green than that sold here, gray hearthstone, slate, grinding stone—mostly red—cobble and paving stone, an abundance of bluestone of various grades suitable for millstones or walling or sculpting, since they differ in hardness and workability; also material closely resembling alabaster and marble, and so on.[61] Because the country is not yet full of people, these things are little regarded, but they could become important as the population grows and splendor and luxury increase, as is the usual consequence.

Of the Paints and Dyes

The indigenous dyestuffs of New Netherland may be conveniently classified into two sorts, to wit, dyes derived from stones and those prepared from plants and herbs. The natives, as repeatedly mentioned, paint their faces and bodies various colors, the one stranger and odder than the other, according to their fancy. To that end they have and usually carry with them small leather bags, each containing a different dye, such as red, blue, green, brown, white, black, and yellow, etc. The most precious and sought after of these is the dye that glitters the most and shines as though it were filings of some refined metal. As recounted above, the dyes that were tested in 1645 had such a gleam. Most are made from stones, which the Indians know how to pound and rub together so as to pulverize them. They regard such dyes as generally superior to those made of plant material, though from certain plants the Indians are able to extract beautiful, bright, and pleasing colors that differ little from stone dyes in effect, except that the metallic gleam is absent. To fully explain just how the Indians prepare all their dyes is impossible for me; they inform me that stony dye material is first pounded and then rubbed between stones, but whether they add some fatty substance I could not say. I do know that most of their stone-based dyes feel fatty and greasy.[62] Most of the dyes of vegetable origin are produced by one method, and in order not to detain the reader too long, I shall describe one that I myself have observed in that country; the others can be approximately inferred from it. A certain wild plant grows there, in appearance like goosefoot, but thicker and producing many shoots from one clump. It bears reddish brown striped berries, which the Indians pick and crush.[63] They take big sheets of tree bark, about six feet long and three feet wide, and pour the juice squeezed from the crushed berries on the inner, or smooth, side of the bark, which is always somewhat concave and turned up at the ends by the sun. This they put out in the sun to dry, but if that takes too long for them or they want to move on, as they often do since they rarely sojourn long in one place during summer, they heat "pounding stones" [*kapsteenen*] in a fire and fling them on the bark into the juice, and thus they can dry it in a hurry. Then they pack the dried residue, now like a hard and firm substance, in small bags and use it as and when they wish.[64] This dye is the most beautiful and brightest purple that I can recall having seen in my life. The Indians dilute it with water so that it sparkles. If it were prepared in a modern way, it would no doubt be a much admired color. The paintings done by the Indians do not amount to much. Most of it is on their bodies and faces and also on the skins they wear. In their large and permanent houses, within the castles and settlements, one may find an occasional portrait painting, but far from creative and subtle.[65] They likewise paint their shields and war clubs as well as the lattice work in their houses, and they can depict in paint ships, trees, and animals.[66] This also is devoid of all charm. One thing I have seen among them I mean to record here, and it is worth telling. The Indians use as finery, instead of plumes, a certain most decorative kind of hair, some of it very long and fairly coarse and stiff, others shorter and very fine. This they have a way of shaping and dressing so nicely that they are a splendid sight when made up with it. The hair is tied with bits of string in the shape they fancy, then dipped in certain dyes they prepare for the purpose, giving it such a beautiful bright red color so that all who see it are amazed. The dye fixes well in the hair, rendering it full and stiff so that rain and wind cannot wear it off or make it fade. On the fine hair the dye takes even better than on the coarse. It also has a remarkably beautiful shine and luster. Although the Indians are able to produce it without any particular skill, such a red has never been made in this country, nor can it be made from any vegetable extract. It was shown here to several renowned dyers and experts in that art; they thought very highly of it and admitted frankly that no one in this country could make such a red, asserting that if that color were known here it would be much prized.[67]

Of the Animals in New Netherland

We will now treat of the cattle and animals, both those taken to New Netherland by the Christians and those that are native to the country, and we begin with the domesticated animals. Livestock was taken across from here at the time of settlement and differs little in build or otherwise from that in the Netherlands. Most of the horses we have there are of the proper breed for husbandry. They were taken from the bishopric of Utrecht and shipped across, and they breed true to the same nature and size. There are also many English horses; they are not so suited to husbandry, being of a lighter build, but are fit for training as saddle horses. They do not cost as much as the Netherland kind and are more freely obtainable. Horses from Curaçao and Aruba are occasionally brought in, but they do not easily take to the country because they are unaccustomed to the cold, which causes their death in winter or at least puts them at risk if they are not very well looked after. Horses in general breed well there and live long, and are not plagued by many diseases, except that one notable pest sometimes causes havoc among them. A horse catching it goes quickly from health to death; it is as though the horse had a stroke, it walks like a drunken man, falls to the ground, and, help seeming to be of no avail, it dies suddenly. This has set people thinking, and some now have a treatment that preserves the horse's life, so that the peril is no longer as great as it was. The origin of the disease is in dispute, which suggests that no one knows the true cause, but all agree that sound veterinarians—so plentiful in some places here that they have little to do, but scarce in New Netherland—could probably discover the cause of the ailment and find a remedy. The regular breed of cattle in New Netherland are the Holland breed. They do not usually grow to the same size they attain here, because the hay is not so nutritious and often the heifers are allowed to mate in their second year, the sooner to

33

have the benefit of increase. If they were to mate at the proper time and were well cared for, as is the practice in Holland, they would become as robust and yield as much as they do in Holland. The Holland cattle [in New Netherland] tend to suffer from illness when feeding on sweet pastures or sweet hay. This caused much loss at first before people knew how to deal with it, but the disorder is now prevented by giving the cattle salt or brackish water or feeding them hay grown on salt wetlands.[68] Cattle were also brought in from the bishopric of Utrecht, purchased on the high ground around Amersfoort. It has been found that they do equally well as the Holland cattle. They are not as big, but yield enough milk, breed well, and are highly suitable for fattening up, because they put on a lot of fat. There are also English cattle, though not brought over by the Dutch but bought from the English in New England. They thrive just as well as the Holland cattle, need less attention and looking after, and can fend for themselves outdoors throughout the winter, as in England. As against that, they do not grow as big as the Holland breed, are quite a bit lower-priced, and yield no great quantity of milk, though it is creamy and has a high butter content. Those wishing to practice cattle breeding and acquire the best strain of cattle should take a bull of the Holland kind to English cows. This produces an excellent crossbreed at low cost. Oxen also render good service and are used for cart and plow, not only by the English but also by some of the Dutch. Stock feeding is going well, and both oxen and other cattle kept for slaughter soon gain flesh as well as fat. Hogs are also plentiful there and are bred and kept in great number by those living out in the country near woods and marshes. Some prefer English hogs, because they are hardier and subsist better outdoors in winter, but ours grow bigger and heavier and produce more bacon. In some years acorns are so abundant in the woods that the hogs gain a handbreadth of bacon by it. When it is not a good year for acorns or the farmer has no access to them, the hogs are fattened on corn, or Turkish wheat. By common consent the bacon thus produced cannot be bettered and surpasses the Westphalian kind; when it is as much as five, six, or seven fingers thick, as happens, its consistency is such that it creaks when cut. Those seeking rapid increase of hogs make sure that the sows get to the boar about Christmas, then the pigs come in April, when the grazing is best. The young follow their mother to the woods and forage there, and when the young sows are a year old, they produce young ones in turn, so that the hogs in New Netherland are numerous and abundant. Sheep are not so many in New Netherland. They are more plentiful in New England, where more attention is given to sheep farming because the weavers' trade is actively promoted, which our Hollanders are not so intent on. Among us the sheep do put on enough fat, so much so, as I have seen, that it becomes excessive and unsightly. They thrive, are in good health, and enjoy enough space and pasture for feeding, also good hay in winter. But because they must be herded and guarded in the fields against wolves and other perils, for which we cannot easily spare men, and also because venison is plentiful, sheep are thought to be in limited demand. There is another circumstance that I think is the main obstacle to a greater stock of sheep. In New Netherland most of the land is wooded, that is, everywhere covered in trees, shrubs, and brushwood. When the sheep wander among and through the bushes, they lose much of their wool as they go. Now wool should be the chief reason for keeping sheep in such countries, but the yield at shearing time is much less than might be expected. Goats are preferred to sheep over there, and they appear to thrive at least as well. Once sheep are fat and are then allowed to become lean again, their health suffers, but this does not apply to goats. Goats also yield a fair amount of milk, which is always in demand. It suits beginning planters of small means to start off with goats instead of cows, because little money is required, the goats breed twice as fast, and the rams, if castrated young, can be readily sold. The meat is delicious. The Netherlanders also have chickens of various kinds, as in this country, as well as capons, turkeys, geese, and ducks. Likewise, pigeon fanciers keep several strains of pigeons. In a word, domestic animals of every description are found there, without exception, down to cats and dogs. The latter are as good as any for training as hunters, gun dogs, and retrievers, making it unnecessary to import dogs.

Of the Wild Animals

Although the winter cold purges New Netherland fairly well, many lions are nevertheless found there. They have never been seen alive by Christians, even by those who have traveled widely throughout the country, and are known solely from the skins of the females, which the Indians very occasionally bring to market. When questioned, the Indians report that the animals are caught in very high mountain ranges far away at fifteen to twenty days' travel to the south or southwest, and that the males are too quick and fierce to be caught.[69] Bears are also to be found in that country, not the gray or tawny ones of Muscovy or Greenland, but mostly with shiny and pitch black skins suitable for making muffs. Though numerous, few are ever seen by the Christians, owing to the bears' keen sense of smell. As soon as they smell a human being, they flee. Therefore the Indians, when setting out to hunt bears outside the hibernating season—of which more later—impart Esau's odor to their bodies and clothing, that is, they apply the scent of field and forest so that they will not be betrayed by a contrasting scent.[70] Bears are sometimes seen by the Christians when they are to the windward of the latter or are swimming across some watercourse, as they often do. Bears are harmless unless attacked or disturbed, as by attempting to shoot or catch them, for then they defend themselves bravely for as long as they can. Anyone planning to shoot a bear ought to be careful, and before he shoots mark out a tree up which he can hastily retreat. If he merely grazes the animal and fails to kill it outright, as is likely, because bears are very tough and hardy, he is in great danger. The wounded bear at once takes a wad of leaves or anything else near him—I shall describe this in detail to the interested reader the way I heard it from huntsmen speaking from experience—and with it plugs the wound, and storms toward the rifleman or the spot where it saw the smoke rise. Meanwhile the hunter should be in a tree, and it must be a thick tree with many branches to baffle the bear or it will also climb up. If the hunter in his tree is adroit enough to finish the bear off, he is all right, but it may be that he cannot and will have to sit and wait until the beast's wrath subsides and it has gone away, which may well take a couple of hours. The bears in New Netherland feed not on carcasses or carrion, as in Greenland, Muscovy, and elsewhere, but on grass, herbs, nuts, chestnuts, and acorns, which they even pluck from the trees—so the Indians tell us. Christians, too, declare that bears climb up trees to eat the fruit, and when they want to come down again, they hold the head between the legs and, no matter how high up they are, they simply drop down and go on their way. Bears are also shot out of the trees. The Indians as well as the Christians of New Netherland state that in winter the bears hibernate for twelve weeks, as follows: In the fall the bears grow very fat, and throughout winter they eat nothing but lie down on one side with a paw in the mouth, sucking it and growling. After six weeks they turn over on the other side and carry on as before.[71] For hibernating they normally choose an overhanging cliff in the mountains, a den, or a dense thicket with many fallen trees, so as to be out of the wind and in safety. According to the

Indians, most bears are captured then, when it is easiest. The heaviest and biggest bears found there, to judge by the skins and the biggest alive I have seen, are the size of an average heifer. They are very fat and may have a layer of fat up to six or seven fingers thick. The Indians consider them good eating, mainly the offal and the head, and the paws are much prized. I have never tasted it, but was told by Christians who have that is it good and tasty fare, as good as the best bacon or pork. Elk are also fairly numerous there and stay mostly to the southward, where few people go. They are very good to eat, and many think the meat more appetizing and desirable than deer, though it has a coarser grain. The tanned skins are rather heavy and are good for making into jerkins. Some feel that these animals could be domesticated—the males, if gelded, and the females if kept in milk and herded with the cows. They are not skittish or intractably wild by nature, and persons who have kept them for fun and broken them in from young find that they become quite tame and easily forget their native forest habitat. This would be even more so and work better by gelding and keeping them among the cows, it is thought, [and] also that the females ought to be covered by a bull, as this would likely produce a good breed of cattle well suited to work, being strong by nature. The breed should also be good for fattening up, seeing that in their wild state they put on much fat, and could be good milk producers. The same persons maintain that such a new crossbreed of domestic cattle, being semi-indigenous, would accord particularly well with the country's condition and be adapted to its nature.[72] Deer are incredibly numerous. Although the Indians kill many thousands throughout the year, principally in the fall, when they are fat, and wolves cause havoc among the newborn deer, yet the whole country is full of them, with no signs of decrease; rarely can one go out into the open country without seeing at times a few and at other times whole herds of them.[73]

The meat is good for household use and makes a tasty meal. It can be had quite reasonably; a fair-sized deer goes for not more than five guilders and often less. Then there are white deer and fallow deer and others of a blackish hue.[74] The Indians say that wherever there is a white or fallow deer, a great many other deer congregate that are attracted to it, but with black deer it is the reverse, they reckon. So the Indians say; a true report we have not so far had from any Christian. There are also other kinds of large animals, but not so many and not normally seen by our Christians, except those from Canada, who relate many strange things about them. I have been told by a Jesuit, whom I met as a result of his having been captured by the Mohawks and released by our Netherlanders, that in Nova Francia, or Canada, they have numbers of woods' oxen, known in Latin as *Boves silvestres*.[75] These are about as big and stout as horses, with a neck like a camel's with long hair like a horse's mane on top, a short tail, and cloven hoofs. They are not wild or predatory and resemble elks in character.[76] I have often heard from the Mohawks that deep inside the country there are animals that seldom show themselves, resembling a horse in size and shape, also cloven hoofed, and having in the middle of the forehead a horn one and a half or two feet tall. Since they are fleet of foot and strong, they are hard to catch or snare. I have never seen any evidence but do believe they exist, because Indian hunters attest unanimously to it, while certain Christians say they have seen the skins, though not the horns.[77] Many wolves also exist there. They are not as big and ferocious as those in the Netherlands and will not usually attack any but the smaller animals, that is, deer—mostly the young ones—young calves, sheep, goats, and hogs. With these last they stand little chance when the hogs are together in a herd, because they defend themselves and help each other. In winter, with snow on the ground, wolves are able like hunters to encircle and catch deer, but need to be eight or ten in number to do it. A lone wolf will sometimes pursue a deer until it tires and is caught. If the deer can meanwhile get to water, however, the wolf loses its prey, for the deer enters the water, but the wolf dare not follow and must stay on the bank, looking on. The fact that wolves drive deer into the water and that deer when chased take to the water if they can, leads to many of them being caught by persons who live where they overlook rivers and water or happen to be on it in a boat. If the deer is close enough to the shore to be intercepted, those in pursuit row toward it and shout. It seems that the echo coming from landward, where the shore often is high and covered in trees, frightens and heads off the animals, which think that the voices come from the land toward which they are swimming, so that they turn back or swim along the shore of the land they are afraid to enter, and so they meet their doom. Some are of the opinion that hunted deer aim only at fresh water, but we have found that in New Netherland they go for any water, and when pursued on islands or places near the coast they run into the open sea, sometimes swimming far out and not thinking of turning back. New Netherland has many beavers, of which we shall treat hereafter; very beautiful and superb brown otters, fine fishers, and bobcats, known in the Netherlands as *loesen*, whose skin is like that of a lioness, and so is their shape, but smaller, and the tail is as short as that of a hare or rabbit.[78] Then there are foxes, and also *espannen*, which in the Netherlands are called *schobben*.[79] The fur of the latter is very warm and beneficial in case of an injury or sprain. When roasted, the meat is good to eat, but because it contains much fat, it is too rich when stewed. They [*espannen*] are easy to capture. They seldom leave the hollow trees where they store their winter provisions other than to drink, but give themselves away by their scratches and traces on the tree bark outside. Having been located, they are brought down with the trees, from which they emerge as though drunk and dazed by the fall, and that is the end of them, to the benefit of the hunter. [There are also] minks, hares, and rabbits. In our settlements the only rabbits are either tame ones or those that have escaped and run wild, but in New England wild rabbits occur. The civet is about the size of an average cat, has a long hairy tail, and smells so powerfully of musk that one can hardly bear being near it. Even when the skins are quite old and dried out, they retain the scent, as do all things that have been in contact with them.[80] [There are also] martens and black and gray squirrels. Some squirrels can fly for several rods, having a filmy skin between the front and hind legs on either side that they spread wide and open up, and so glide as quick as a flash to wherever they want to be. There are also woodchucks, badgers, *trommelslagers*, and other species with which we are unacquainted or have not seen, and some which we have seen but do not know their names; therefore, we move on.[81]

Of the Avifauna, Aquatic and Terrestrial, and First the Raptors

The birds of prey in New Netherland are many and of various kinds. Among them are two species of eagle, so different that they do not resemble each other at all. One is the ordinary kind, as often seen and well known in this country and elsewhere. The other is somewhat bigger and the plumage is much browner, but all of the head, part of the neck, the whole tail, and the flight feathers are white as snow, which makes them very attractive and delightful to look at. Over there they are called whiteheads and are fairly common.[82] There are also falcons, hawks, sparrow hawks, swifts, kites, and many other raptors that we are unable to name, but all are bent on mischief.[83] They eat nothing but fish and flesh of whatever kind they are best at catching. These birds could well be trained and used for the hunt, as may be inferred from their innate ability to choose their quarry wonderfully well, in that the smallest of them always aim for small prey, and the medium-sized ones or those that reckon they are strong enough, look out for starlings, thrushes, blackbirds, grouse, and suchlike, each according to what it thinks it is best able to overpower.[84]

Eagles are after more substantial quarry and inspire awe wherever they are to be seen. As a rule they keep to areas where the forest is old and, therefore, not very dense, and near shores and big rivers where they can survey the fish, swans, geese, and ducks that are their main prey. These fowl do not always catch by their own effort, unlike the fish that they snatch alive from the stream. When a bird has been wounded or grazed by a hunter, the eagles are promptly there, even though none was seen in the vicinity by human eyes; they glide high up in the air beyond our ken, always scanning the terrain for prey. Where eagles tend to be, no or very few black-birds and other birds that ruin the crops will be seen. Eagles relish the flesh of deer and continually scan the ground for where a wolf has surprised and caught a deer and has abandoned or partially eaten it. They can spot it while on the wing. People who are aware of this have followed such gliding and circling, which is usually at no great height, and so got to a deer that had been savaged and halfway eaten by a wolf. It also happens that hunters wound but fail to bag animals, which then die from loss of blood, and thus, whole and undamaged deer are found. There is another raptor, whose head is like that of a big cat and whose plumage is pale gray.[85] No name for it is known in the Netherlands, but Director Kieft presumed to know and said that in France it is called *grand dux*. Also that the bird is highly prized by the nobility there, who are the only ones to use it; that, though difficult to train, it excels at hunting once it has become habituated to it; and that it sells for one hundred French crowns apiece.

The most important other bird life of the country are the turkeys, which are similar to those in the Netherlands. They are to be found throughout the woods, mostly in the fall and winter, in great flocks numbering twenty, thirty, forty, fifty, and more. Turkeys can grow enormously big and heavy, up to twenty-eight or thirty pounds. I have heard of, but not seen, some weighing thirty-two pounds net, dressed and ready for the spit. The wild and tame turkeys hardly differ in taste, but fastidious folk prefer the former. We have often bought turkeys, when at their best, from the Indians for ten stivers each, while among the Christians they usually went for about a *daalder*.[86] Turkeys are occasionally caught with dogs in the snow, but most often they are shot. This is done at night because turkeys sleep in trees, whole flocks of them together and in the same place most nights. Having observed the place, a couple of huntsmen or more go there and likely come home with a dozen or two fowl. The Indians catch them in winter toward year's end with snares, making use of a certain bulb that comes up in rills and streamlets and is favored by turkeys; when they eat it, they also swallow the barb [implanted in it] and must stay put to await their captor.[87]

Partridges of various kinds are also found there, some smaller than in the Netherlands and some bigger. Specialists already have various names for them and are very particular about it. People in this country cannot believe that partridges fly up and perch in trees, so that they are often shot down from there, as I and a hundred others have more than once done and seen. I have heard that someone in the colony of Rensselaerswijck once shot and collected eleven grouse out of a flock that had perched on a stockade, such as are commonly used to fence and secure land. Near fences one can find small partridges, which are very tame or stupid and dense, for they may fly straight into houses or run across roads and gardens between everyone's feet. They also startle people by flying against the chest or body, so that many are killed with a cane or stick.

Then there are woodcocks, moorhens, grouse, pheasants, wood snipes, water snipes, etc.[88] Also flocks of cranes, many of which are shot on mowed land in the fall and are good fare.[89] Herons, bitterns, and many pigeons, very similar to wood pigeons, come flying over twice a year in such tremendous numbers and big flocks that they are as clouds in the sky, shrouding the earth in shade while the sun shines and covering the ground where they land. At those times, in the spring and the fall, many are shot, both on the wing and in the trees. They alight in masses on the trees, mostly on dead trees to have a better view, and from there they can best be brought down without the foliage obstructing the aim. On the ground, too, many are shot, and it is nothing to wonder at for twenty-five at a time to be dispatched with one shot. The Indians or natives can find the places where the pigeons hatch, and push the squabs from the nest with long poles. At such nesting sites the pigeons flock together in enormous numbers of countless thousands, such that the Indians with their wives and children move there often in groups of hundreds and stay for as long as a month, eating little else but squabs, which, as mentioned, they push from their nests with poles.[90]

The quails have a different call and also differ in size quite a bit from those in the Netherlands. The woodpeckers have fine multicolored plumage and a big crest. People call them *boompikkers*, because that is what they do, and with such force that from afar in the woods it seems as though someone were knocking on the trees with a wooden mallet.[91] I have seen trees in which they had pecked big holes and then built a nest inside.[92]

Blackbirds are also very numerous. The name they are given there fits their deeds: corn thieves. They are so set on this that when the corn is ripening it must be closely guarded and protected, or they swoop down on it in dense masses. They are too bold to be scared away by gunfire.[93] Only in places frequented by eagles are the blackbirds less a plague. I have been told as the truth by reliable persons that one Jacob van Curler once shot and killed 170 with one shot, not counting those he wounded or which escaped.[94] From this anyone can judge their numbers.[95]

Then there are ravens, crows, owls, swallows, sandpipers, etc., and smaller species such as various kinds of finches, kingfishers, house wrens, white throats, and winter wrens.[96] Among them are songbirds, warbling out in the open, and some are beautifully colored. I have seen birds there of an azure color that gleamed brightly; also yellow ones with a roseate tint, and some all-over orange in a brilliant flame color, other than a black bill and a few black flight feathers.[97] Finally there is a curious little bird whose nature—whether it is a bird or a West Indian bee—is in dispute. We shall leave the dispute aside and simply describe the bird's shape and habits. It is slightly more than the length of a finger, not counting the beak. The tail is a thumb's breadth at its widest, and many of its feathers have a beautiful glint to them. The little beak and the two tiny legs are like other birds. As far as can be observed its beak is not used for pecking or eating; it sucks from flowers everywhere in the manner of bees, and its beak is shaped for that purpose. That is all it lives on. Therefore, people say it is a West Indian bee, since it is seen in New Netherland only in summer during blossom time, and it makes a buzzing sound like a bee. They are very delicate and could not well be kept in captivity. Some people spray water on them and dry them between two sheets of paper in the sun, to make a present for a friend.

Particularly abundant in New Netherland are waterfowl. They are to be seen mainly in the spring and fall seasons—there are far fewer at other times—and then the rivers and waters are teeming and alive with them; indeed, people living nearby are often unable to sleep owing to the birds' whirring and squabbling. Among the principal species are the swans, the same as in the Netherlands and as big, and in season there are so many of them that the riverbanks and bays where in the main they congregate are covered with swans and appear quite white.[98] The geese are of three kinds; the first and best are gray and are therefore known as gray geese.[99] They are bigger than any in this country, and not as big as swans, and do much damage to the wheat growing near the shores inhabited by them. Some people think these birds are actually bustards, but that cannot well be credited, for there are too many of them. A great many are shot, and they are incomparably better for the table than the other kinds. I knew a sharpshooter by the name of Herry de Backer who prided himself on having shot eleven geese at once out of one dense gaggle. The other varieties are the blue goose and the white-fronted goose, some of the latter being entirely white like those here.[100] These birds keep to the seashore in dense flocks during cold weather, and many are shot, often eight or ten in one volley. A certain planter, Jan Virginis, to my knowledge once shot and bagged sixteen geese with one shot, apart from those that were wounded and swam off.

Of ducks there are several kinds: pintails, teals, and widgeons. Also loons, shovelers, cormorants, and several strange species, some of which are said to be pelicans, and other waterfowl that we pass over as being of little importance. If there were people in that country familiar with decoy fowling, they could do a good business and have a rich catch. Though fowls are cheap now, that would improve with an increase in population, and there are the feathers as well. Such persons would have to lay out next to nothing for the site and the fowling rights.

Of the Fish

Practically all the waters and rivers of that country abound in fish. In the rivers, according to season and locality, we have sturgeon.[101] It is not valued and seldom taken as food when full-grown. No one takes the trouble to salt it for profit, and the roe, of which the precious caviar is made, is not utilized at all. Salmon exist in some places, and the *twalift* are everywhere. The latter fish I can compare by its appearance to nothing closer than the salmon, from which it differs only in that the salmon is red inside and the *twalift* all white. It is good eating and some people are particularly keen on the head. The *dirtienen* is not comparable to other fish we know, other than that it is a fairly good fish, easily as long as the cod but not as bulky. I heard while I was there that this fish got its name at the time when our Christians first began fishing there and everyone was intent on seeing whether they knew the fish being caught, and if they did not, on giving it a name. At first much shad [*elft*] was caught and, a little later in the year, the *twalift*, for as the shad get fewer, the *twalift* make their appearance in large numbers. This fish was new to them, so they named it in sequence *twalift*, followed by the *dirtienen*, since they come out somewhat later and were named accordingly, and those names they are said to have retained from then on.[102]

Next we have carp, bass, pike, trout, minnow, silverfish, sucker, tadpoles, flounder, *aal, paling, brikken*, and lampreys—some as thick as a leg and more than an ell or an ell and a quarter long.[103] The sunfish tastes exactly like the perch but has a spotty skin of brightly flecked scales, fine like those of the perch, and that is why it bears the name of sunfish. In falls of fresh water, during winter, one occasionally finds a fish

43

that comes up from the sea and has the appearance and taste of mullet. Some believe it is silver hake. It is tame enough to be grabbed by hand, and because it appears when frost sets in it is called frostfish.[104]

Out to sea and also in some parts and bays of the East River, cod are plentiful. If people were to go in for it on the basis of the experience that has been gained, shiploads could easily and cheaply be had nearby. Also present are haddock, jellyfish, herring, mackerel, ray, flounder, plaice, and sheepshead. In shape and taste the sheepshead resembles the sunfish, except that it is much bigger and not spotted. It is as heavy as the very biggest carp that are on rare occasions seen here. The teeth in the front of its mouth are like a sheep's, though it is not snappish.[105] Another species, known as the blackfish, is much relished by the Christians. It is as brown as the dace, shaped like a carp, but the scales are not as coarse, and when served at table—as happens often, for they are available throughout summer—it goes down very well, because everybody likes it.

Then there are seals, tuna, dolphinfish, and the like, and in some places from time to time, also whales. These are not being caught, yet if ships were fitted out [for whaling] the catch in nearby waters could be quite adequate. The stage has not yet been reached in the country, however, for such matters to be properly taken in hand. Meanwhile, there washes up on the beaches here and there some stray creature or other whose name cannot even be guessed.

Lobsters are found in many places, some very big, up to five or six feet long, others of a foot and a half, and these are best for the table.[106] Crabs vary in size, as in this country. Some have no shell and are soft all round. They are called soft crabs and are very useful when cut in pieces for baiting fishhooks. Further, gurnards and seahorses; also various conch shells, washed ashore in masses by the sea at certain times of the year, and of which the Indians make their *sewant*.[107] A large

44

quantity of fine oysters are found in many places, some small like Colchester oysters or a little bigger, which can be eaten raw; others quite large and occasionally containing a small pearl. The large oysters are brownish in color and not worth much, but are fine for stewing and frying. As each one fills a big spoon, they make a good bite. I have seen several that in the shell were a foot long and correspondingly wide. The usual price is six to eight stivers a hundred. Mussels are plentiful and of different kinds, and there are also cockleshells, mother-of-pearl shells, periwinkles, and similar things, not all of which I can put a name to. Also shrimps, and tortoises—both in the water and on land. Some people use the turtle, which is the larger, to prepare savories, but to me they are too tart and raw tasting.

Finally there are sea spiders and various other forms of marine life unknown in these parts. They are of small account since they are of little use to the human race.

Of the Poisons

During my residence of eight or nine years in that country, I never learned of more than one poisonous plant growing there. It is called the poison earth chestnut and bears little resemblance to the earth chestnut. Its blue flowers are attractive and grow in clusters like cardinal flowers, or poppies, as they are called in Brabant.[108]

There are also snakes of different species, among them a black snake and a mottled one, in the water and on land.[109] They are said to crossbreed with eels. Some are rainbow-colored underneath, and none does any harm beyond eating eggs and preying on young birds. They always flee from humans, who usually kill them if the snake tarries too long. The Indians are not at all afraid of them and will run after a snake, catching it first by the tail and then by the neck so that it cannot move its head; then they crush the neck with their teeth or sever it halfway, the blood trickling from their mouths, as I have seen with my own eyes, after which they throw the snake down and leave it to die. There is also a small snake of about the length and thickness of a tobacco pipe. It is not often seen and keeps to tall brushwood. Many are of the opinion that it could do harm, but I have never been able to ascertain as much.

Rattlesnakes, like those in Brazil, occur as well. It is hard to describe what they look like to anyone who has never seen this snake or a picture of it. Many maintain that the fiery serpents that plagued the children of Israel in the desert were of this kind, but that is not certain. They are, in any case, nasty vermin and will not lightly give way to man or beast. The rattlesnake is brightly patterned in yellow, black, and purple, and has a thick head with four long, sharp fangs, which the Indians use as lancets. The body is shaped like that of other snakes except for the tail, which holds the rattle.[110] This consists of a hard, dry, horny substance in overlapping sections, with which they can rattle loud enough to be heard from several rods away. They rattle only when angry and ready to bite, nor do they bite without rattling. Then they vibrate the tail with the erect rattle at the end, and the motion makes a noise. The rattle grows by one button each year; some believe by half a button, and since the buttons are double, this would make one whole button every two years. Rattles of six or seven buttons are encountered often, but I have seen one there of fourteen buttons; that was most unusual. When the rattlesnake is about to bite, it is hideous to look at, as I have experienced on a stick in order to observe its motions closely. The snake widens its head, opens its mouth wider than one would expect, and snaps fiercely. At the same time as it bites, a blueish skin that lies folded against the palate opens out and from it venom oozes down along the upper teeth into the wound. The venom looks like a blueish salt. If one is bitten by one of these creatures and the venom enters the wound, one's life is in danger. I have known this to happen to some persons, though they came to no grief, but others break out all over in stripes and colors like those of the snake that bit them. The Indians themselves dread the rattlesnake very much, and some die of its bite. The best that can be said of this snake is that there are not many of them, and unless a person were constantly out in the fields, he may spend seven years in that country without encountering one. A certain herb known as snakeweed grows there, which is effective protection from rattlesnakes, because they perish as soon as they smell it.[111] This was tried out on a big rattlesnake that lay in a plantation on Long Island. [The people there] took a long stick, spat chewed snakeweed and spittle on it, and at a distance held it under the snake's nose. No sooner did it get the scent of it than it shivered like someone who catches a chill and expired where it lay.[112] The Indians value this herb very much, and some always carry it with them.

There are small adders as well, but I have never heard of them doing harm. Some of the lizards are as in this country, and others have azure tails.[113] The Indians are terrified of them, because, they say, when asleep in the woods, the lizards will crawl into their bottoms and cause them to die a miserable death. When I add the toads, the foregoing is what I have been able to learn of poisons and venomous animals in that country.

Now, as promised, we must treat of the winds, air, weather, and seasons, proceed to the natives, and then return to the beavers.

Of the Wind

The swift messenger and foster mother of commerce, the wind, blows in New Netherland from all points of the com-

pass, without the regularity of monsoons and trade winds.
In winter the cold weather most often comes with northerly winds, and in summer south and southwesterly winds prevail. In the depth of winter calm days are the rule, as in this country, particularly when it is freezing hard, as it often does. Then it is not easy to tell which way the wind blows and not a leaf stirs, so that whichever way one turns the wind seems to move toward one. The northwester, though, which brings most of the cold air, is very sharp, violent, and persistent, other than near high or steep mountains, where at times it drops.

Thunderstorms there can be expected in spring, with an easterly wind from the sea at spring tide. They seldom go on for more than three days, and if the wind veers a little toward the south, as frequently occurs, it blows steadily and brings warm and hazy air or rainy weather. The west wind is more vigorous and blows strongly, with frequent showers. Since throughout the country this wind blows mostly over water, however, and at sea the shore is then to windward, it holds no danger. North and northwest winds bring cold weather, as east and northeast winds do in this country, and though it may be mild with a southerly breeze, a northerner may spring up, and in a few hours the weather changes completely to cold. This wind is very strong and penetrating, but since at sea it blows from a windward shore, it is seldom reported to cause damage, except in the woods, where it blusters briskly and fells or breaks many trees. Then is the right time for the hunter, for amid the rustling, creaking, and crackling he can get close to the game.

The sea washes the south side of the land, and no severe weather normally is to be expected from that quarter, other than at spring tide with an east wind, as mentioned. In summer a pleasant sea wind blows on most days at flood tide, and, wafting over the cold element, it brings cool and refreshing air. On calm summer days it is quite hot, and squalls are likely.

These rise in the west or the southwest, carry on blithely for one, two, or three hours, then it clears from the northwest and the air turns lovely and cool. Often, within an hour's time, it may look as if it will rain cats and dogs, and the next moment there is not a cloud in the sky. Far inland, easterly winds are rare, sometimes fewer than once a year; it seems they are deflected or obstructed by high ground.

Of the Air

The gentle governess of mind, strength, and form alike in humans, animals, and plants is the air, also termed the temperament or climate. The air in New Netherland is as dry, pure, and wholesome as could be desired, and so clear, agreeable, and delicate as would be hard to match anywhere else. It occasions surprise in New Netherland when, in that salubrious climate, someone is sickly or in failing health. Many people who are not at their best, whether in the West Indies, Virginia, or other parts of the world, soon feel as fit as a fiddle when they come to New Netherland. In short, Galen has a lean time of it there.[114] Thick vapor or foul fog there is none to speak of, and if anything harmful were to come up, a northerly wind soon disperses and dissipates it, and leaves the air marvelously pure. On account of its wholesome climate, therefore, the country has much to commend it.

The heat is bearable and in the hottest part of summer is often tempered by a sea wind, a northerly breeze, or a shower. The cold is more severe than the climate seems to suggest and, owing to the keen air, sharp and penetrating, though always dry when the wind is from the north. Nature indicates the right defense: to dress so as to withstand the cold. In humid weather the cold never lasts long, for such weather rises from the south, and as soon as the southerly air prevails the cold is gone, even in the depth of winter. It can even happen that the south wind, if it persists, brings mild and warm weather as though it were spring. The humidity is seldom oppressive, nor does it continue for long. Yet there is plenty of rain in season, more in some years than in others. It pours down freely, seeping down to the roots, and quite soon the weather is fine again and the sky clear. Thunder and lightning, which are common in warm weather, thoroughly cleanse and clear the air. For the rest the weather depends, with exceptions, on the time of year.

Of the Seasons

The yearly round of the seasons and the measurement of time in New Netherland are as in the Netherlands. Although the two countries are on quite different latitudes, [the former being] more southern, they differ proportionately much less in high and low temperatures. To state the matter more precisely, one should know that winter generally ends there in February—we refer here in general to the situation at New Amsterdam, the heart, head, and center of New Netherland. Thus spring weather comes in March, and the spring season is reckoned from the twenty-first of that month. Rarely does it freeze hard later than that or does summer weather arrive earlier. Then all of nature bursts free, fish dart forth from muddy depths, the trees bud, and the grass sprouts. On many farms the cows go to pasture in March, on others they must wait awhile yet; that varies from year to year, but horses and poultry are always allowed out. By May the grass is green, and the trees are in full foliage. April is the proper month for gardening, and on the fields, too, sowing should not be delayed. If one is not quite ready for it, sowing can also be done later and there will be enough time left for the crop to ripen.

48

Most of the changeable and turbulent weather occurs at this time, especially with spring tide and an east wind, which may drive the sea up against the shore but will not cause flooding. Those who are keen to see the country have now, in April and May, the best opportunity. Grass and brushwood do not yet clog up the forest, there is fodder for the horses, the cold is gone, and the burning heat is yet to come. Cleared by bush burning, the land is now most accessible, the trees are in flower, and sweet scents pervade the forest. By mid-May, without fail, we have ripe strawberries, not in the gardens, where they are not planted, but growing naturally in the fields; they might ripen even earlier if cultivated in gardens. Summer arrives quite suddenly there, since the warm weather, when it comes, builds up quickly. Grass and herbage respond as fast: in a matter of eight or ten days all of the land can change from brown to green. Frost does not occur as late as in this country. It is surprising to hear of it in May; rather, the month of May takes us straight into summer, for then the winter wheat blooms and is at full height.

Summer might as well begin in May but is reckoned from June so as not to make it too long. The summers over there are usually quite hot and seldom so rainy that it becomes tiresome, and we can fairly say that, taking one year with another, the summers are always better than in the Netherlands because they are more equable. The rain seldom lasts long and tends to come as a squall or a thunderstorm, which we have often and are used to in summer. It goes on for one, two, or three hours, or half a day; if it rains for three hours on end everyone is amazed, and it hardly ever continues beyond that. The rain causes no damage but is rather looked forward to, as there is much high ground. The soil is porous and absorbent, so that water does not remain standing and is soon soaked up. An isolated summer storm may wet the soil down to root level, yet it is followed in the twinkling of an eye by a northwester that clears the sky as though no rain had ever fallen. Heavy dewfall in dry periods, which does occur as well, greatly refreshes plants and herbage. Now the fields yield their annual interest, and the trees gladden the eye; only the tobacco and the vine often await the month of September. In the streams the fish rejoice, and the cattle gambol in the fields. No one wearies of the summer, however long it may seem, before it draws to a close, for in that season man and beast alike enjoy its bounty everywhere.

The days over there are not so long in summer, nor so short in winter, as in this country. They are shorter in summer and longer in winter by one and a half hours in both the morning and the evening; that is, in summer the days are three-quarters of an hour shorter in the morning and the same amount of time is lost in the evening; correspondingly, in winter the sun rises three-quarters of an hour earlier than in this country and sets as much later in the evening. This difference is found to cause no inconvenience whatever, as the summer days are warm and long enough to complete whatever one wishes to do or to amuse oneself, while in winter the time always seems to have flown before one fully realizes it. To examine in detail the cause [of this phenomenon], and the opposing arguments, would exceed our purpose, and we leave that to the learned; we simply state for the benefit of ordinary people the general and most likely view, which is that New Netherland is situated nearer the equator or more in the center of the world than this country is. While varying in length, the days and nights differ even more in sunrise and sunset: one and the same day and daybreak that we have and enjoy here, we always have and enjoy in New Netherland about six hours later, so that at twelve noon here it is found to be not later than approximately six o'clock in the morning there. Regarding this there are again several arguments, which it would take too long to recount in full. Most say that this is from no other cause than that New Netherland lies so far to the west; others go further and dispute the roundness of the globe. Here we note merely the actual situation, which no one disputes and which has been frequently verified from the difference of the eclipses.

The autumns in New Netherland are normally as fine, lovely, and pleasant as could be desired anywhere on earth, not only because the fruits that awaited the passing of summer now yield up their treasure and the fields their surplus, but mainly because the season is so well tempered as regards heat and cold; and the weather it brings is fine and lovely as though it were in the month of May. Though some mornings may be a little hazy, the haze is dispersed by the rising sun before ten o'clock and is not malodorous or unwholesome, so that it causes but little inconvenience. Also, leaves, grass, and herbage that had perished, withered, or been trampled during the summer sprout anew, as in springtime, to the delight of men and beasts. Not much rain falls in autumn, just some brief showers, and the rain seldom goes on for as long as two or three days on end. For the rest the weather is fine and wonderful day after day, with bright sunshine and moderate temperatures. In short, the autumns there are lovely and more pleasant than the summers are here. They are also quite long; away from the highlands and near the coast winter is hardly felt before Christmas, that is, until then there is little frost, the waters remain open, the sun shines every day, and the weather is fairly warm. In many places the cattle may be kept in the fields, mainly during the day. Northward, in the highlands and the freshwater region, cold and freezing weather may occur so that the cattle must be stabled.

Now is the time to stock the larder and prepare for the coming winter. The fattened oxen and hogs are slaughtered, and geese, turkeys, and deer are at their best. They are also easiest to obtain, because the waterfowl keep inshore owing to the cold and the woods have been burned over in many places. This is the Indians' real hunting season, and so many deer and suchlike are killed that a person who did not know the country's nature and extent would judge on the face of it that, within a year, all would be destroyed. Since the country is so extensive, however, and thus provides abundant subsistence for the animals, which can only be hunted in a few and limited areas, no decrease is observable. The Indians tell us that when they were still in full force and number, before and for a while after the arrival of the Christians, for since then their numbers have dwindled owing to smallpox and other causes to the extent that there is now barely one for every ten, then, correspondingly, many more animals were hunted and killed, and nevertheless, neither increase nor decrease has been noticed.[115]

The winters in New Netherland vary appreciably, both from year to year and according to the place under consideration. Thus it is to be noted that throughout the highlands, toward the colony of Rensselaerswijck and the area extending inland to New England—which we reckon to be part of New Netherland, as in truth it still is—the winters are quite a bit colder and longer than in New Amsterdam or the coastal districts such as Long Island, the South River, and nearby places. This area is seldom in the full grip of winter and frost before Christmas. Though some night frost and snow flurries may come earlier than that, it does not amount to much, and by day the weather is mostly fine. In the colony of Rensselaerswijck, however, it has been known to freeze over earlier, as happened in 1642, when the river closed on November 25 and remained frozen for a long time. Lower down and near the coast that never happens so early; there, as mentioned, the frost keeps off until Christmas or even later, and the rivers seldom freeze over completely. They do get full of ice floes so that navigation is impracticable and remains so for as long as the wind is from the north, but when the wind turns south or east, the ice rapidly vanishes from the water. Thus it may happen two or three times in a winter that ships can sail for a while and then must be laid up again.

Much rainy weather or a strong wind blowing persistently from one quarter are not common or expected there in winter. It seems, and many argue thus, that owing to the rarified and thin air, moisture is transformed by the cold into hail or snow while still contained in the clouds and before it approaches the earth. This may all the more readily be credited because the winter season brings much snow, which in the highlands can remain on the ground for weeks and even months without thawing away entirely. Below that region the south wind is stronger, and the snow cover does not last, melting before the wind every time it blows. Once or twice in a winter, when frost follows rain, the trees may become coated with clear hoarfrost, which is a remarkable and delightful sight as it flickers in the sun, particularly on forested mountain slopes. Some people maintain that heavy hoarfrost presages a good fruit crop for the coming summer.

It is astonishing and almost inexplicable that New Netherland, situated on the same latitude as Spain and Italy and as hot in summer, is yet so cold in winter, despite the near absence of wind in the coldest period. The cold is also drier than in this country, which lies much farther to the north. Hence, trees, plants, and herbs that are not resistant to cold are unsuitable [for cultivating there]. On the other hand, pelts and furs actually surpass those of Muscovy in beauty and quality. Various reasons for this difference are given, which we shall briefly pass on to those interested, if only provisionally and without prejudice, to anyone's views and opinions, since the many arguments advanced are for the most part uncertain. Some declare it is because New Netherland lies so much farther down the westward slope of the globe; others refute this, and point to the similarity of the summer weather to that of Spain and Italy, and to the view that the earth is flat and that New Netherland lies at the far edge of it. In support of the latter opinion they ask how, since the fourth and last-discovered continent is roughly the size of the other three together, the earth can still be thought of as round after about half was added to it. Others again state that the higher one ascends, the thinner and colder is the air, and as New Netherland is situated very high toward the west, it must be so cold in winter and can still be so warm in summer. The most probable explanation given by many is that this land extends several hundred miles to the north and northwest and finally abuts on a frozen sea. Serious doubts exist about the last point, however, since the Davis Strait would have to be navigated, which has not yet been done. Between the high and steep mountains of those far inland regions, the snow remains on the ground or seldom thaws, so that when winter winds blow over it the air is cooled both from above and from below and, therefore, brings severe cold. If it were otherwise, they ask, how can it be that when the wind blows from the sea, even in the depth of winter, it is warm and mild as though it were spring.

The cold is not so severe, however, as to be harmful and hard to bear; in many respects it is desirable and beneficial in that it clears the land of vermin and removes all pungent and injurious vapors. It also firms up the skins of bodies and plants and improves their fitness. Moreover, nature very providently relieves the discomforts that accompany the cold. For one, abundant wood is available everywhere to be taken and used at no charge; and for another, the land yields excellent returns and produces enough foodstuffs for the people to share with all the world. Indeed, even the Indians, who do not wear the thick clothes we do and go about half naked, withstand the cold well and have no fear of it, nor are they ever overcome or noticeably harmed by it. On bitterly cold days, perhaps, they will not disport themselves in the open so much. Then it is mainly the women and children who do, as the men are not so keen on it, except in summer or on warm days.

OF THE MANNERS AND EXTRAORDI-
NARY QUALITIES OF THE ORIGINAL
NATIVES OF NEW NETHERLAND

Their Bodily Shape, and Why They Are Called *Wilden*

Having briefly spoken of the attributes of the land as far as needful, it will also be worthwhile to treat in the following the nature of its original natives, so that when the Christians shall have multiplied there, and the Indians melted away, we may not suffer the regret that their manners and customs have likewise passed from memory.

In figure, build, and shape of the body, both men and women are equal to the average and well-proportioned sort here in the Netherlands. In height, and as well as between height or weight and girth, they vary as elsewhere, the one less, the other more, and seldom deviate from the average. Their limbs are nimble and supple, and they can run strenuously with striking stamina, carrying big and heavy packs with them. They are very good at all voluntary physical exercise when so inclined but quite averse—chiefly the menfolk—to heavy sustained labor of a slavish type. They arrange all their tasks and affairs accordingly, so that they will not need to do or work much.

Congenital defects and deformities are very seldom seen among them, and in all my time in that country I never encountered more than one who was born with an unsound body. Cripples, hunchbacks, or otherwise misshapen persons are so rarely seen that one may in truth say that such do not exist there, and if one does occasionally observe a maimed or infirm individual, it will appear upon inquiry that the defect resulted from an accident or was inflicted in war. All are slender and clean limbed, and none is particularly heavy, fat, or gross. Although generally speaking, nature has not endowed them with surpassing wisdom, and they must develop their best judgment without formal training, yet one finds no fools, madmen, maniacs, or lunatics among them. Both men and women tend to be broad shouldered and slim waisted. The hair of the head, before it is changed by old age, is always jet black, quite sleek and uncurled, and almost as coarse as a horse's tail. Any other color or kind of hair they regard as conspicuously ugly. On the chest, under the arms, and on the chin and the private parts of the body, they have no or very little hair; any hair that does come up sparsely in the said places they pluck out at the root. It rarely regrows, other than on old men, some of whom are a little stubbly here and there around the chin. All, men and women alike, have fine faces with black brown eyes and snow white teeth. Purblind or cross-eyed persons are very seldom found among them. Of those born blind I have never heard or been told, and they seldom lose their sight by accident. I have known of only one with cataracts on both eyes, whom smallpox had left blind. In great old age their sight fails, but not as early as in this country.

The hue or color of their bodies is generally not as white as ours, though some quite fair-skinned ones are to be found, and most are born white. The rest tend toward a yellowish complexion like the Gypsies or heathens who roam through our country, or like the country folk who are much in the open, as they are, without guarding against the sun and the air. Their yellowness is no fault of nature, but only an acquired feature due to the heat of the sun, which burns more powerfully than in this country. Passed from generation to generation, the effect is all the stronger. Despite the yellowness they all share, some more than others, one finds many handsome and graceful persons and faces among both men and women. It is true that at first sight they appear somewhat strange to our people, because color, speech, and dress are so different, but for those who associate with them frequently the strangeness soon passes. And it seems that their womenfolk have an attractive grace about them, for several Dutchmen, before many Dutch women were to be had there, became infatuated with them. Their countenance and facial features are as theirs and as varied as in this country, seldom strikingly beautiful and even more rarely very ugly, and if they were instructed as our women are, they would no doubt differ little from them, if at all.

The original natives of that country—for there are now also many natives not originally from there, but Christians born of Christians—were all called *wilden* by our people as a general appellation, though they are divided into many different tribes. That name, as far as can be ascertained, was given them from the first and is quite appropriate for a number of reasons. First, on account of religion, because they have none or so little as to be virtually in a state of nature. Second, as regards marriage and in the recognition of landed property, they deviate so far from the general laws that they may well be called *wilden*, because they act in those matters almost at will. Third, as the Christians, to set themselves apart, give foreign nations the names of Turks or Mamelukes or barbarians, since the term *heathen* is too general and little used abroad, they did not wish to include the American natives in that term either. Similarly, the terms *black* and *white* are customary among those who have business overseas, to distinguish the Negroes from our and similar nations, but neither of those names quite fitted the Americans, who tend toward the olive colored. Therefore our people, on the spur of the moment rather than with forethought, it may be supposed, called them *wilden*, as the first name that occurred to them. And since the first opinion of women and the uneducated is best, it seems appropriate that they be called *wilden*, because they are quite wild and are strangers to the Christian religion.

Fare and Food of the Indians

In food and drink, even on their feast days, the Indians are not at all excessive, wasteful, frivolous, or lavish, and [are] easily contented so long as they have something to keep body and soul together and satisfy hunger and thirst. Nor is it customary among them, as it is with us, that the highest placed, the noblest, or the richest expects to be treated accordingly and better than a poor devil or a common man, but always and everywhere their food and drink are sufficient and, according to season, the same for all. Their usual drink has always been water, from a fountain or a spring if they can get it, as they seldom fail to do. When they are well provided, they will occasionally drink grape juice, if it is in season, with fresh meat or fish. They drink the juice fresh and never turn it into wine. Beer, brandy, or strong liquor are unknown to them, except to those who frequently move among our people and have learned that beer and wine taste better than water. The Indian languages are varied and rich, yet none has a word denoting drunk. Drunkenness they call madness, and to drunken men they refer as fools, such as those few who associate often with our people or are otherwise able to obtain liquor, for most of them have no taste for liquor at all. In order to prevent insolence, the government has forbidden the sale of strong drink to them. They drink greedily in getting drunk and are then just like Saint Valentine in his cups, as the saying goes.[1] Before they become accustomed to alcohol, they are easily made drunk, a small beer or two being enough to

55

do it.[2] But in time they learn to tolerate liquor equally well as the Netherlanders do. Gout, podagra, pimply and red noses, or similar afflictions are unknown among them, as are drink-related accidents.

Their food is normally fish and meat of every kind, depending on the time of year and the locality where they happen to be. They have no pride or particular fashion in preparing and serving these, and cook fish or meat simply in water without any herbs, salt, or lard, other than may be naturally present in it. They are also ignorant of stewing, braising, baking, frying, etc., and rarely heat or grill anything, unless it be morsels of meat and small fish when traveling or hunting and having to make do. For bread they use maize, or Turkish wheat, mills being unknown to them. Their women beat or pound it, as the Hebrews did their manna in the wilderness, and bake cakes of it. They will also add the grits to meat to make a broth, the way some use barley or rice here. But their common fare for which this grain is most used is porridge, known there as *sappaen*.[3] Its use among the Indians is so general that rarely a day passes without their eating it, unless they are traveling or hunting, and one can hardly ever enter an Indian dwelling that this porridge is not being eaten or prepared. All of them, including women, children, and old people, are so attached and used to it that when they visit us or one another they first of all ask and look for *sappaen*. Without it one cannot entertain them to their liking, nor can they, so it seems, eat their fill. It is often cooked together with meat or fish when available, mostly not fresh but dried and pounded into meal. They do this toward the end of winter and the approach of spring, when the hunting season is past and their stock of provisions is nearly exhausted. They also eat a lot of Turkish beans, which they consider a delicacy when boiled with fresh meat in plenty of water.[4] Further, they take as food and sustenance all sorts of meat, fish, and fruit that the country yields and they can obtain.

They do not observe customary or fixed meal times as our people usually do and judge it best to eat when they are hungry. They have tremendous control over their appetites, stomachs, and bodies, so that they can get by with very little for two, three, or four days. When supplies are ample once again, they will quickly make up for the loss or delay, yet this does not upset their stomachs or make them ill. Though good eaters, they are not gluttons. Ceremonies of seating at the upper or lower end of the table, being the first or last to partake of a dish, or to be served or waited upon, I have not been able to notice. Except on the major festivals, they very seldom invite one another, but those under their roof when mealtime comes around will be served as well. No one is passed over, and it is not their custom to accept payment. Exceptional treats for their guests are beaver tails, fatty meat, rockfish heads, and roasted corn pounded into meal over which is poured a fatty broth.[5] Also [considered treats are] chestnuts boiled for a while, shelled, crushed, and prepared by stewing in gravy and fat.

When they intend going on a long journey to hunt or to wage war, and know or surmise they will not find supplies, they provide themselves with parched meal made of roasted corn. Such meal goes far and is nourishing so that a small bag lasts them for many days. Less than a quarter of the contents is used up in a day because it is so concentrated and swells out again when moistened. They carry the little parcel with them, and when hungry they take a small handful from it and drink some water and feel themselves well enough looked after to carry on for another day. If they can get some meat or fish to go with it, the cornmeal serves as a slice of bread and needs no baking.

Of the Dress and Ornaments of Men and Women

Most Indians wear the same kind and shape of clothing and are not showy or luxurious in that respect, except for some young lads, who soon forget about it when they grow older. The women are more inclined to adorn and decorate themselves than the men are, though they do not go to nearly the lengths seen in this country. The young males up to twelve or thirteen years of age go about quite naked; the girls generally cover their private parts as soon as they begin to walk. Around the waist they all wear a belt made of leather, whale fin, whalebone, or *sewant*.[6] The men pull a length of duffel cloth—if they have it—under the belt, front and rear, and pass it between the legs. It is over half an ell wide and nine-quarter ells long, which leaves a square apron hanging down in front and at the back. It suits them well, is quite comfortable, and also airy in summer, when they often wear nothing else. It covers their nakedness and hence bears the name of *Cote*.[7] Before duffel cloth was common in that country, and sometimes even now when it cannot be had, they took for the purpose some dressed leather or fur, cut it like such a cloth, and made it fit. Our people everywhere refer to it by the vulgar name of *clootlap*, which word may appear unseemly to some in this country, but this shows that words simply have their usage, and in that country it is such that the word does not offend the ear of delicate women and maids.[8]

The women also wear a length of woolen cloth of full width and an ell and a quarter long, which comes halfway down the leg. It is like a petticoat, and under it, next to the body, they wear a deerskin, which also goes around the waist and ends in cleverly cut pointed edging and tassels. The wealthier women and those who have a liking for it decorate them entirely with *sewant*, so that such an undergarment is often worth between one hundred and three hundred guilders. As covering for the upper part of the body both men and women use a sheet of duffel cloth of full width, i.e., nine and a half-quarter ells, and about three ells long. It is usually worn over the right shoulder and tied in a knot around the waist and from there hangs down to the feet. By day it serves them as a cloak, and by night as a bed and a blanket. Men's and women's stockings and shoes are of deer or elk skin, which some decorate richly with *sewant*, but most wear them as they come. Some of them also make shoes out of cornhusks, but those do not last.[9] Some now buy their stockings from our people, and that appears to suit them best. The men mostly go bareheaded, and the women tie the hair at the back of the head and fold it into a tress of about a hand's length, like a beaver tail. Over it they draw a kerchief, often exquisitely decorated with *sewant*. When they want to appear splendid and lovely, they wear around the forehead a strap of *sewant* shaped like the headband that some believe was worn in antiquity. It holds the hair neatly together, is tied in a bow to the tress behind, and so makes quite an elegant and lively show. Then around the neck they wear various trinkets mostly made of *sewant* and regarded by them as very fine and elegant, as pearls are among us. They also wear many bracelets of *sewant* around their wrists and prettily wrought figures on the breast, which is halfway and not closely covered.[10] Many of them drape beautiful belts of *sewant* around the waist and wear pretty little ornaments through the earlobes. The women and maids, even when decked out in their finest and smartest, paint their faces little or not at all, other than a small black beauty spot here and there, and present a very stately, quiet, steady, and yellowish appearance from which all playful coquetry seems to have been banished, more so than it really is.[11] The men are painted all over, though mostly the face, in all kinds of vivid colors, so that when one is not accustomed to seeing them thus, he does not recognize them. And when it is parade time, they look so stately, proud, and self-possessed that they will scarcely deign to turn their heads. Some wear in addition a circular headdress of very long and fine deer hair, dyed red, rather like the halos that used to be painted over the heads of saints, and which looks very handsome. They further have short plaits of fine and shiny hair hanging over the chest.[12] When a young fellow is dressed up like that, he is almost too haughty to open his mouth. They seldom adorn themselves to that extent, however, with the exception of a few maidens in the flower of their years. At other times all of them are by nature dirty and careless of their persons.

In winter, when it is cold, the women and children especially do not often leave their shelter. As was mentioned, they cover themselves with duffel cloth, and some wear it folded double. They further shield their bodies against the cold with bear and *espannen* fat rubbed on the skin and by wearing a jerkin and sleeves of bear skin. They also have clothes made of the skins of weasels, bears, deer, and elk, in which they can withstand the winter quite comfortably. In a word, they have the necessary clothing to cover their bodies and withstand the cold, but also know how to dress up for show and formal occasions. White linen used to be unknown to them, but many are now beginning to look for shirts and buy them from our people; they tend to wear the shirts without washing until worn out.

Their Houses, Castles, and Settlements

Most of their houses are of one and the same shape, without special embellishment or remarkable design. When building a house, large or small—for sometimes they make them as long as a hundred feet, but never more than twenty feet wide—they stick long, thin, peeled hickory saplings in the ground, as wide apart and as long in a row as the house is to be. The sapling poles are then bent over and fastened one to another, so that the frame looks like a wagon or an arbor as are put in gardens. Next, strips like split laths are laid across the uprights from one end to the other. On large houses the strips below are laid rather closer together than on the roofs, and upward in proportion until they are a foot or so apart. This is then covered all over with very tough bark. For durability everything is peeled so that no worms can get in. Then they go out and get the bark of ash, elm, and chestnut trees; if it is late in summer, rather than peel those, they take instead white cedar growing near the waterside, whose bark yields easily even when the others are dry. With such pieces of bark of about a fathom square, the smooth side turned inward, they cover the entire wooden frame, the cross members of which are up to a foot apart near the top, as has been stated, and lash the bark down securely where needed. If there is a hole or tear in the bark, they know how to plug it, and against shrinking they lap the sheets of bark. In sum, they arrange it so that their houses repel rain and wind and are also fairly warm, but they know nothing about fitting them out with rooms, salons, halls, closets, or cabinets.[13]

From one end of the house to the other along the center they kindle fires, and the space left open, which is also in the middle, serves as a chimney to release the smoke.[14] There may be sixteen or eighteen families in a house, more or less according to the size of the house. The fire is in the middle and the people on either side. Everyone knows his space and how far it extends. If they have room for a pot and a kettle and whatever else they have, and a place to sleep, they desire no more. This means that often 100 or 150 and more lodge in one house. Such is the arrangement of a house as they commonly are found everywhere, unless they are out hunting or fishing, when they merely put up a makeshift shelter. In the villages and castles they always do solid and good work.

As sites for their castles they prefer a high or steep hill near water or on a riverbank that is difficult to climb and often accessible on one side only. They always make them flat and even on top. This they enclose with a heavy wooden stockade constructed in a peculiar interlocking diamond pattern. First they lay a heavy log on the ground, sometimes with a lighter one on top, as wide and as broad as they intend to make the foundation. Then they set heavy oak posts diagonally in the ground on both sides to form a cross at the upper end, where they are notched to fit tighter together. Next another log is laid in there to make a very solid work. The palisades stand two deep and are strong enough to protect them from a surprise attack or sudden raid by their enemies, but they do not as yet have any knowledge of properly equipping such a work with curtains, bastions, and flanking walls, etc. They also build some small forts here and there on the level and low land near their plantations to shelter their wives and children from an assault, in case they have enemies so nearby that they could be fallen upon by small parties. They think highly of their forts and castles built in that fashion, but these actually are of little consequence and cause them more harm than good in a war with the Christians. In such a castle they usually put twenty or thirty houses of up to a hundred feet and some even longer, like those measured by our people at up to 180 paces. Seeing that they manage with so little space in the castles, as related above, they cram such a multitude of people inside that it is unbelievable and leaves one amazed when he sees them come out.[15]

Besides these castles they have other settlements that lie in the open in the manner of villages and often have the woods on one side and their cornfields on the other. They also have settlements at certain places near water where they are in the habit to do much fishing every year and at the same time plant some crops, but those places they leave toward winter, when they remove to the castles or dense woods where it is warm and firewood is close at hand. There as well no wind can trouble them, and they have good opportunity for hunting, by which they nourish themselves in place of fishing. They seldom abandon their secure castles and large settlements completely, but otherwise they easily pack up and move on. They seldom remain long in one place and follow the season and time of year. That is, in summer, when the fishing is good, they move to the watersides and rivers; in fall and winter, when meat is best, they seek the woods. Sometimes, but mostly in spring, they travel in droves to the seashore to eat oysters and to stock up on all kinds of shellfish, which they know how to dry and preserve for a long time.[16]

Ways of Marriage and Childbirth

Having covered bodily shape and care, dress and ornaments, and described the communal dwellings, we shall now indicate the consequences without which all that was related before would come to naught, that is, marriage and its consequences. Since it is the only sustenance and continuation of all the world, no nation is to be found anywhere so primitive that does not benefit from its effects and has not retained some of its features. In New Netherland, among the original natives—for among our people it is the same as at home—one can still just perceive the early traces of marriage, but if this is to be improved it must be done soonest. The words *man* and *wife*, *father* and *mother*, *sister*, *brother*, *uncle*, *aunt*, *niece*, *nephew*, *married* and *single* are well known and usual among them, and this is a sure sign, even if no other evidence or more direct proof could be furnished, that something resembling marriage exists. To speak more clearly, the Indians do marry, and usually but one wife, except for chiefs or rich and powerful persons, who may have two, three, or four at the same time, generally of the handsomest and most diligent. It is remarkable that they, guided only by the light of nature, so manage their womenfolk that one never hears or can learn on inquiry that any hatred, quarrel, or discord prevails among these women, or arises over the upbringing of the children, domestic affairs, and preferences regarding the husband, in which respect they follow his pleasure alone.

Weddings are not nearly as ceremonious as among decent people in this country, and the "everyman" of the Indians can have it as casual as he likes. They observe no definite marriageable age and judge this by competence alone, which they are not loath to try out beforehand. The marriages of young folks who are acquainted through mutual kin are normally arranged with the latter's knowledge and advice, with regard to family and standing. In the case of widowed or separated persons, of whom there are many, it is not usual to involve kin. The man, according to wealth and condition, must always present some gift or tribute to his future bride, like the wedding coin of old, as a token of their mutual pledge. But if a widow or a widower were married without the counsel of kin and they afterward disagree, or one of them *buyten de pot pist*, or some other misunderstanding arises, the husband often takes back his belongings and banishes his wife from his bed, and if she does not leave by herself, he turns her rudely out of doors.[17] For among the Indians no marriages are so firm and binding that they cannot be dissolved at once and completely by one or both parties, whenever the wife or the husband wanders or some misunderstanding causes disaffection. It is indeed in those parts a common and usual occurrence, so much so that I have known men who habitually changed wives every year, sometimes for little or no reason. One sees as well that when a marriage breaks down or marriage partners are changed, it is the husband's doing more often than the wife's. In a divorce the children follow the mother; many nations reckon descent accordingly, also for greater certainty. All the same, the longer the spouses stay together and keep their marriage vows, the more laudable and honorable that is held to be.

During marriage, prostitution and adultery are considered

most disgraceful, particularly among the women, who would rather die than consent to it. They think it even more vile when done by the light of day or in open fields where someone might watch or the sun shine on it and, as they say, sees it. No man will keep his wife, however much he loves her, when he becomes aware of such conduct. If the woman is single or otherwise unattached, however, it does not matter and she may do as she pleases, provided she accepts payment. Free favors they regard as scandalous and whorelike. She is not blamed for what else happens to her, and no one will later scruple to propose marriage to the woman concerned. It also happens that a free woman cohabits with someone for a time so long as he satisfies her and gives her enough, whom she would nevertheless not wish to marry. They are actually proud of such liaisons and as they begin to grow old, boast of having slept with many chiefs and brave men. I was amazed to hear how sedate and steady women, of the worthiest among them, thought highly of themselves when speaking of such conduct on their part, as if it were praiseworthy and glorious. When a girl reaches marriageable age—they speak of her as ripe—and, still being single, is desirous of marrying, she covers head, face, and body all over, leaving no skin exposed, as a sign of her purpose. Then generally one after the other presents himself and proposes to her. That is the usual procedure over there, even for girls who in any case have enough suitors but yet wish to proceed in that manner in order to make their intentions known to everyone and so likely improve their prospects, seeing that the men folk rarely propose in vain.

When pregnant, whether in or out of wedlock, Indian women guard very carefully against anything that could injure the unborn child. They seldom experience bad or painful days during pregnancy. When their time is near, which they estimate fairly closely, and they fear heavy labor or it is their first confinement, some of them take a potion of local roots and herbs. Then they commonly go into the woods, though it be the depth of winter, where they give birth unaided. For this they prefer a quiet, sheltered spot near running water where they put up a simple hut or a screen of matting and the like, having brought some provisions with them. If the child is a boy, they immerse it straightaway in the nearby *killetjen* or stream and leave it there for some time, even in freezing weather.[18] The child must be hardened from the first, they say, so as to grow up a brave man and a good hunter. Then they dress the infant and wrap it in warm fur clothing and keep a close watch on it lest it die accidentally. After spending a few more days in that place, they return to their home and family. It is curious that confinement causes them no illness or any lasting indisposition, nor do they die in childbirth. The reason given by some is that they have less knowledge of good and evil than we have and are also less sinful, since labor pains are not natural but are a punishment for sin imposed on the first mother. Others hold that it is due to the wholesome climate, their well-formed bodies, and their general coarseness.

Of Suckling, and the Relations between Men and Women

It is unknown in that country for women to have their children breast-fed or nursed by others. They all, of whatever rank, do so themselves. This is true in and around New Amsterdam to a distance of a few days' travel, but I am told that farther inland some women are not so particular. While suckling or with child the women will not consort with men, simply for the reason they themselves give, that it would harm the infant or the unborn child. During this time they are not so strict if the husband sees another. But as for themselves, they keep strictly to their rule and consider it shameful and scandalous for any woman to do otherwise. Nor do they see this as a reason for weaning their children early, since they normally continue breast-feeding for a year. During the time of their impurity as well, they are averse, distant, and shy, keep apart and seldom appear or let themselves be seen by men. Only if it comes upon them during some festivity, gathering, or social occasion will they excuse themselves and depart, if at all possible, without returning before it has passed. At other times, though, when all is well and they are unattached, they make light of their virtue, both men and women being extremely liberal and uninhibited in their relations. Foul and improper language, however, which many of our people think amusing, they despise. Kissing, romping, pushing, and similar playful frolicking, popularly known as fondling, and other suggestive behavior one is unlikely to see among the Indians. They speak scornfully of it when done in their presence. And if they see Netherlanders behaving in that fashion, they tell them sarcastically, "Shame on you; if you are so inclined, wait till nighttime or when you are alone." Could anything be funnier? Yet at the right time they will decline no proposition, and almost all of them are ready to play the whore and carry on with abandon. Some, who have two or more wives, as do chiefs and prominent persons, will readily accommodate a visiting friend with one of their wives for a night, but if it happens without their knowledge, they resent it and repudiate the woman or, as they say, send her packing.

Ways of Burial, Lamentation, and Mourning

When someone among the Indians departs this life, all around take great care in committing the dead body to earth. Even though the deceased was a complete stranger, having no friends or relatives there and hardly known to anyone, they do not neglect the usual ceremonies. If he was a person of some standing, they observe the same customs, with variations according to his position. During the terminal illness they all give faithful support, but once the soul has parted from the body, it is the closest relatives who come to straighten the limbs and shut the eyes. After a few days and nights of vigil and lamenting, they carry the corpse to the grave, where they do not lay it down but seat it supported by a stone or a block of wood as if sitting in a chair.[19] Then they place money, a pot, a kettle, a dish, and a spoon, with some provisions, next to it in the grave in case, they say, the departed has need of it in the other world. Next they stack as much wood around the corpse as will keep the earth away from it, and over the grave they build a great mound of wood, stone, and earth with a wooden enclosure on top like a little house. All the places of burial are secluded and held to be sacred, and it is to them a serious offense or villainy to disturb, damage, or desecrate such places.

The closest relatives observe a set period of lamentation. It is mainly the women who do, for the men seldom show outward signs of grief. The women call out the name of the departed with hideous howling and strange gestures, beat their chests, scratch their faces, and display every bodily sign of mourning. When a mother has lost a child, her lamenting exceeds all bounds, for she wails and rants whole nights through as though she were stark mad. If the deceased died young or fell in war, the lament is adapted to it. The mourners shave their heads and burn the hair on the grave at a specific time in the presence of kin. In sum, they are much affected and upset by someone's passing, particularly if they were related or close to that person. Also, in order to put the mourning and grieving behind them all the better, and not to afflict the memory of the deceased's kin, together with all those of the same family, jurisdiction, and those living in the same area and carrying the same name, they dislike making mention of it, talking or asking about it, and feel that doing so is meant to hurt and injure.[20] Mourning attire is not usual, other than by close kin, and then only in the form of a few black markings on the body. When a woman's husband dies, however, she shaves her head and blackens her whole face, as a man does when his wife dies, and wears a deerskin waistcoat next to the skin. They mourn and do not remarry for more than a year, and even if they were recently married or had not been happy together, they observe these ceremonies very strictly.

Their Festivities and Special Gatherings

Feasts and grand dinners are not regular events among them but are sometimes held to deliberate on peace, war, contracts, alliances, and agreements. Also to consult the devil on some future matter or outcome, or on the crops and the fruitfulness of the year; or else to rejoice at a good outcome with dancing and merriment.[21] Peace or war with neighbors and surrounding nations are not decided in haste or by the few, but debated in all their councils, where anyone who has any authority is free to state their opinions at such length and as amply as they please without anyone interrupting them, no matter how long the speech or whether it goes against the mood of many. But if they fully approve of what was said, they voice their acclamation toward the end of the address. The councils always meet before noon and do not normally continue beyond noon. If no conclusion is reached by then, they resume in good time in the morning.

When they plan to practice witchcraft, however, and conjure the devil to reveal the future, as is their way, the meeting takes place in the afternoon toward evening. Some of their number are wonderfully able to consort with the devil and perform great magic, or so at least they make the common people believe. They begin by jumping, shouting, ranting, and raving as though they were mad and possessed, light big fires and dance around, beside, and right through them. They tumble and roll head over heels, beat themselves, and perform such queer pranks that they break out all over in a sweat that trickles down their bodies. With such sickening behavior and grimaces they seem to have become devils themselves, so that it is horrible to see for someone not used to it. When properly in a trance the devil charmers start a dismal jabbering and howling and holler at one another as if possessed by demons. After this has gone on for a while, the devil appears to them, so they say, in the shape of an animal; if a predatory animal, it is a bad omen; a harmless animal is better. The apparition tells them strange things in reply to their questions, but seldom so clear and detailed that they can rely on it or fully comprehend it. They learn or appear to learn something from it and grope for the meaning like a blind man reaching for an egg. If the matter turns out differently, it is their fault not to have understood. Sometimes they read more into the message than it contains. Any Christians who may be present can observe the hubbub, but while they are there the devil will not make an appearance. Sometimes the sorcerers can cast a spell on some of the common folk so that they foam at the mouth as if possessed, in a way not otherwise seen, for they throw themselves into the glowing hot fire without feeling it. After a while someone whispers in his ear, and he is once again as quiet and meek as a lamb.[22]

To celebrate some or other success or to dance, they assemble in the afternoon. First a spokesman explains the matter; then they treat one another with food, as may also be done following a council meeting. They are hearty eaters, and everyone consumes so much that it ought to last them for three days. Nothing must be left over; food not eaten there is to be taken home or fed to the dogs. When they have gorged themselves so fully that they can only move their wretched heads, the old and staid have a smoke to round off the feast, while the young and not-so-young take to singing, skipping, and dancing, often the whole night through.[23]

How Human Beings and Animals
First Came to That Country

Various arguments are put forward when one undertakes to investigate how those we now call *wilde menschen* first came to that part of the world, which seems always to have been separated by the ocean from the other three continents.[24] Some say they were settled there, but others ask by whom, and how did lions, bears, wolves, foxes, snakes, and other venomous and harmful creatures get there? No one would carry such creatures in ships for the purpose of transplanting them. In discussing the creation with the Indians, we have never been able to satisfy them or give them answers they believed.

Many think, with reference to an unknown chronicler, that long ago in legendary times a group of people sailed well equipped from parts of Sweden and Norway to look for a better country, led by a chief named Sachema, and that it has never been determined where they ended up. And since all the chiefs in New Netherland who live by waterways and seashores are known as *Sachemaes*, it is concluded that they descend from those settlers.[25] That conclusion is not easy to accept, but the matter remains puzzling.

Others advance the view that the people of that part of the world did not originate with Adam and that a separate creation of humans and animals took place there. Many reasons are given purporting to prove that no deluge passed over those lands, which are represented as a completely new world that differs in all respects from the old. That is true enough, but from another perspective.

The same persons also trouble their heads over the question whether on doomsday, when all the world ends, the new world also will be judged. They argue that its population is of recent date and for the most part innocent; that portion of the globe is not so accursed and defiled by sin and therefore will not incur the same just punishment as the more sin-laden rest of the world.

Then there are some who say that probably in ages past, the sea between Cape Verde and America was narrow, even narrower than between Calais and Dover, so that people and animals were able to cross from Africa to America by way of the islands. That is hard to believe; but if not there, they add, it was elsewhere. The latter seems to us the best-advised view, the more so as certain studies show that the Chinese visited Brazil and that along the indented shore of the Strait of Magellan or somewhere on the other side of America, a narrows or contiguity of land existed. For the peopling of America must necessarily have happened by migration and not by creation, or the very foundation of Scripture would be destroyed. Those of a contrary opinion ask, if America could actually be seen from Cape Verde or thereabouts, did Petrus Columba [Christopher Columbus] and Americus [Amerigo Vespucci] discover what had never been lost? To pursue these disputes is not to our purpose, however, and we leave everyone his freedom to judge and to write more on the subject.

Of the Different Nations and Languages

The variety of nations, tribes, and languages in that part of the world is as great as in Europe. Those of one tribe or nation tend to keep together and have a particular chief and their own form of government. There are also higher chiefs, to whom the others submit. All appear to have sprung from one original stock, however. They will not lightly marry into another tribe, for each is jealous of its strength and tries to increase its numbers. Just as tribes, settlements, and places have their chiefs, so has every house. He who is the most prominent and respectable of each such community has the authority and eminence. Rank is established correspondingly, though not always observed in practice.

Their languages are very diverse and differ as much from one another as Dutch, French, Greek, and Latin. Declension and conjugation resemble those in Greek, for they, like the Greeks, have duals in their nouns and even augments in their verbs. To render their speech in one or other European language is impossible, and they have no taste or inclination for it. Until one makes the effort to learn their language he understands as little of it as if he heard a dog bark. Some omit to sound the letter *R* in their language, but others voice it so often that they hardly utter a syllable without it. Apart from that the pronunciation varies little, and they can mostly understand one another.

Their languages can conveniently be divided into four main groups. Though there are appreciable differences between them, the speakers readily manage to communicate. The divisions are Mahatans [Manhattans/Rechgawawanks], Minquaes [Susquehannocks], Siavanoo [Shawnees], and Wappanoo [Wappingers]. By Matanse [Manhattans/Rechgawawanks] are meant those living in that part along the North River, on Long Island, in Newesinck [Navesink River/Sandy Hook], Achtertoe [Achter Col, Hackensack River/Newark Bay], etc. The Minquaas are those living far inland, like the Maquas [Mohawks] and the Sinnekes. The Siavanoos live to the southward, and the Wapanoos reside northeast of us.[26]

The Indian languages are very seldom learned fully and perfectly by our people, though some, by conversing in those tongues over an extended period, have reached a point where they can understand and say everything. Not being learned men, however, they are unable to teach others or set out the principles of the language.[27]

Of Money and Their Manufacture of It

That there should be no greedy desire for precious metals in that country no one believes who has ever looked the place over. Yet the use of gold and silver or any other minted currency is unknown there. In the areas that the Christians frequent, the Indians use a kind of currency they call *sewant* [wampum]. Anyone is free to make and acquire it, so that no counterfeiters are to be found among them. The currency comes in black and white, the black being worth half as much again as the white. It is made of conch shells, which are cast up by the sea about twice a year or taken from it. They knock off the thin shell wall all around, keeping only the middle standard, or pillar, that is surrounded by the outer shell. These they grind smooth and even and trim them according to whether the pillars are thick or thin. They drill a hole in each, string them on tough stalks, and file them down to equal size. Finally they restring the sticks on long cords and issue them in that form.

This is the only money circulating among the Indians and in which one can trade with them. Among our people, too, it is in general use for buying everything one needs. It is also traded in quantity, often by the thousand, because it is made in the coastal districts only and is mostly drawn for spending in the parts where the pelts come from. Among the Dutch, gold and silver currencies also circulate, and in increasing amounts, though as yet much less than in this country.[28]

The Innate Character and the Pastimes of the Indians

The Indians are notably melancholy, unaffected, calm, and of few words. If a few have a different disposition, that does not upset the general rule. The little they do say is long considered, slowly spoken, and long remembered. When buying, trading, or having other business, they say no more than is necessary. For the rest, they speak of nothing very worthwhile other than concerns their hunting, fishing, and warfare, though the young men will chat to each other about the girls. While not given to gross lies, they are not very careful with the truth or in keeping their word either. Cursing, swearing, and scolding are foreign to them, unless they learned it by mixing with our people.[29] Surpassing wisdom and outstanding intelligence are not encountered among them, merely a reasonable knowledge based on experience. Nor are they keen to learn or diligent in that respect. Good and evil they are quick to recognize. By themselves they are simple and ignorant, but when they have spent some time among our people they become quite clever and [can be] taught anything. They are dirty, slovenly, and careless, with all the faults arising from it; also most vengeful and headstrong, and unconcerned at facing death if it comes to that. They scorn any pain inflicted on them and take pride in singing until they succumb. Avarice and begging are in their nature, and they must not be entrusted with too much or they tend to become thievish. Yet they are by no means upset when refused even a trifling request. Strongly independent, they do not tolerate domination. They resent being struck, unless they have done wrong; then they endure it passively. Delicacies in food and drink do not tempt them. Cold, heat, hunger, and thirst they bear remarkably well, and they disregard hardship.

From the youngest age they swim like ducklings. Outdoors, they spend their time fishing, hunting, and making war; at home, they relax, smoke a pipe, frolic in the brook, or play with reeds, which is to them as keeping company and card playing are with us.[30] Grown old, they knot fishing nets and carve wooden bowls and spoons. The men do no regular work; such work as needs to be done falls to the women.

Their Bodily Care and Medicine

They are completely devoid of expenses whatever and dislike medication and purgatives. When something ails them, fasting is their cure, and if that does not help, they go into *stooven* and sweat it all out.[31] They do this mainly in the mild season of the year and may drink some potion with it, though very little. The *stooven* are made of clay, set into the ground, fully enclosed, and fitted with a small door through which they can just pass. They heat a quantity of pebbles and shove them in all around the sides. Then the patient sits down in the middle, quite naked, cheerful, and singing, and endures the heat as long as he can. Emerging, he lies down in very cold spring water. This method benefits them greatly, they declare, and is a sufficient remedy for various ailments.

Fresh wounds and dangerous injuries they know how to heal wonderfully with virtually nothing. They also have a cure for lingering sores and ulcers. They can treat gonorrhea and other venereal diseases so easily as to put many an Italian physician to shame. They do all this with herbs, roots, and leaves from the land, having medicinal properties known to them and not made into compounds. Of course, nature assists them well in much of this, because they do not eat and drink to excess, else they could not accomplish so much with so little.

When someone falls seriously ill and may die, they go either with everyone or their closest kin to chase the devil and make noise enough to dispatch at once a person who is at death's door. Actually the devil is supposed to reveal, as they would have us believe, whether the patient will live or die; also, what remedy must be used to get him back on his feet in cases where there is hope of recovery. They seldom receive a clear answer, however, and must apply some remedy anyway. If there is hope, the patient is straightaway served food, which he is persuaded to eat heartily whether he feels like it or not.[32]

The Farming, Planting, and Gardening of the Indians

70

The women do all the farming and planting. The men are hardly concerned with it, unless they are very young or very old, when they help the women under the latter's direction. They grow no wheat, oats, barley, rye, etc., are unacquainted with plowing and spadework, and do not keep their lands tidy. Grain for bread and porridge they obtain by planting Turkish wheat, or corn, together with assorted beans, as mentioned earlier. They also plant tobacco for their own use, but of a different variety that is not as good as ours and requires less work and looking after.[33] They have no garden vegetables except for pumpkins and squashes, also discussed earlier. Their plots and gardens are not fenced off from the open field, and they give little attention to them. Nevertheless they raise so much corn and green beans that we purchase these from them in fully laden yachts and sloops. They know nothing of manuring, fallow seasons, and proper tillage. The labor they devote to farming is all manual, using small adzes that are sold to them for the purpose. Not much more is to be said of their husbandry; yet they regard their methods as better than ours, which, in their view, involve far too much bother, care, and effort for their liking.

Special Account of Their Hunting and Fishing

They all have a passion for hunting and fishing and observe set times of the year for it. Spring and part of summer are given over to fishing, but when the game begins to increase in the woods and the early hunting season approaches, many young men quit fishing. The elderly go on longer, until winter and the main hunting season, but do in the meantime take part to the extent of setting snares. Fishing is done in inland waters, except by those who live on the coast or the sea islands and there enjoy special opportunities. They fish with seines, pound nets, small fykes, gill nets, and gaffs. They are not accustomed to salting or curing fish but dry a few for pounding into meal while the fish still smells. In winter, the meal is added to their porridge, as stated earlier.

Youths and fit men like hunting bears, wolves, fishers, otters, and beavers. Deer are hunted and killed in great numbers in the coastal areas and near riverbanks, where most of the Christians live. They used to catch deer only in traps or shoot them with arrows; now they also use guns. What is most entertaining to watch is to see them form a team of one or two hundred, storm across a broad field, and bag much game. They also know how to construct game traps of thick poles joined together, with two wide wings in front and narrowing to a throat at the end. Into this they drive a horde of game and slaughter them.[34] In a word, they are clever hunters, well trained to capture all kinds of game in various ways.

Beavers are caught far inland—for near us there are not many—mainly by the black Minquaes (not because they are black but because they wear a black square on the chest); by the Sinnekes, the Maquas, and the Rondaxkes, or French Indians, who are also called Euyrons [Hurons].[35] The Indians set out on the beaver hunt in big parties that are gone for a month or two, and meanwhile, live on what else they can catch and meal or corn they have with them. They catch as many as forty to eighty beavers each, and other game like otters and fishers as well. All told, an average of eighty thousand beavers per year are killed in this part of the country, not counting elk, bears, otters, and deer.

Some people worry that in time all the game may be exterminated, but there is no need for concern; hunting has gone on for many years, and the yield is not diminishing. The country is full of ponds, lakes, streams, and creeks, and its vast expanse stretches as far as the Pacific Ocean, indeed beyond travel and cultivation, so that the animal life in many parts remains undisturbed.

Distinctions of Birth, Rank, and Quality

Social differences among the Indians are not nearly as great and obvious as among us. They say frankly they are unable to understand why one person is so much higher placed than another, as they are in our estimation. Still, the Indians recognize some as noble born and the others as commoners, and those will seldom marry outside their station. No chief has the power to confer rank; authority and chieftainship are hereditary and continue as long as the chief's family produces persons suited to that rank. A guardian may govern in the name of a minor. The oldest and foremost of the households and families, together with the supreme chief, represent the whole nation. Commissioned rank is conferred in time of war only and on merit without regard to household or standing. Thus the lowliest person can become the greatest military chief, but the rank dies with the person. If his descendants follow in his footsteps, however, they may continue to be accounted noble, and that may well be the origin of the Indian nobility. The nobles themselves esteem their rank highly, though not as much as in this country. The commoners show little respect for rank unless it is accompanied by courage and energy, and then it really counts. Such a person they call Monitto or Ottico, for he is like the devil who is a wizard. [36]

Of Their Warfare and Weapons

The principal order, authority, and structure of command of the Indians is revealed in time of war and matters pertaining to war, but it is not so firm that they can maintain platoons, companies, and regiments whenever they wish. They march in separate files and out of step, even when in their best formation. They attack furiously, are merciless in victory, and cunning in planning an assault. If it is a dangerous one, they operate by stealth, very quietly, and under cover of darkness.

They will always attempt to ambush and deceive the enemy, but face to face on a plain or water they are not particularly combative and tend to flee in good time, unless they are besieged, when they fight stubbornly to the last man as long as they can stand up. Captives are not ransomed, nor can they be certain of their lives before they are handed over to someone who had previously lost a close relative in war. They will seldom kill women and children in the heat of the attack and never afterward. Instead they take away with them as many as they can capture. The women they treat as their own, and the children are brought up as though born among them in order to strengthen the nation. They all fight as volunteers and are not retained in regular service by pay. They cannot pursue a campaign strategy or conduct a siege for very long. The men will not lightly divulge a planned attack to us, but they do tell their womenfolk, and no sooner do these learn of it than they make it known to the Christians—for whom they generally have a liking—if they reckon the operation may hurt them. When some undertaking is being planned or an approaching danger feared, the women and children are removed to a place of safety until the attack has taken place or the danger has passed.

Their weapons used to be, always and everywhere, bow and arrow, a war club on the arm and, hanging from the shoulder, a shield big enough to cover the trunk up to the shoulders. They paint and make up their faces in such a manner that they are barely recognizable, even to those who know them well. Then they tie a strap or a snakeskin around the head, fix a wolf's or a fox's tail upright on top, and stride imperiously like a peacock. Nowadays they make much use in their warfare of flintlock guns, which they learn to handle well, have a great liking for, and spare no money to buy in quantity at high prices from the Christians. With it they carry a light ax in place of the war club, and so they march off.

73

Of Their Administration of Justice and Penalties

The ordinary pursuit, order, and administration of justice, as they ought to be exercised to protect the virtuous and punish the wicked, do not exist among these people, or at any rate to such small extent that the Dutch over there, observing the proceedings with concern, are amazed that a human society can remain in existence where no stronger judicial authority prevails. All personal misdeeds such as theft and related crimes, adultery, prostitution, lying, cheating, false witness, or similar offenses against the law, remain unpunished. This goes so far that, in my time there, I knew of a woman—an unmarried harlot—who did away with her own child, and though it was widely known, nothing happened in consequence. Also, that someone on several occasions violated women whom he encountered in the woods and other lonely places, and nothing was done about it. For the rest I never heard of any serious transgressions during the nine years I was there, other than theft, which is fairly common among them, though not in large hauls; it may be a knife, an ax, a pair of shoes or stockings, and suchlike. If one catches the thief in the act, one may boldly repossess the item and box his ears, but if the loss is discovered later it must be reported to the chief. He will usually return the article to you and sharply reprimand the thief. Even though the chief punishes his subjects no worse than in words, it is incredible how they fear this and how little mischief is done, by and large much less than in our community with its energetic administration of justice.

Manslaughter and injuries to the person concern the chief's and the culprit's kin only insofar as atonement can be made. They not only promote this strongly but will also contribute liberally should the culprit lack the means, as is frequently the case, for manslaughter is not expiated without much money. The closest relative is always the avenger, and if he can get his hands on the killer within twenty-four hours, he slays him in turn and with impunity. If the killer can avoid capture and death for a while, the avenger is protected by the closest kin during that time, but after twenty-four hours have elapsed action is seldom taken. Even so, the killer must flee and stay under cover while kin try to settle the terms of the atonement. These would include that the culprit must keep away from his kin, wife or husband, and children, and turn aside should he encounter them.

It is rare for anyone to be condemned to death, other than prisoners of war infringing the law of nations. Such are sentenced to death by fire and are burned very slowly at the hands and feet so that it takes as long as three days before the sufferer expires. Meanwhile he does nothing but sing and dance right to the end since to scorn pain and suffering is one of the principal virtues they praise and esteem.

74

Of the Universal Law of Nations

Of all the rights, laws, and maxims observed anywhere in the world, none in particular is in force among these people other than the law of nature or of nations. Accordingly, wind, stream, bush, field, sea, beach, and riverside are open and free to everyone of every nation with which the Indians are not embroiled in open conflict. All those are free to enjoy and move about such places as though they were born there.

Safe conduct is not obstructed, and quarter given in time of war is respected, while indefensible sites are spared. They do not break a pact they have concluded, even with enemies, except with great reluctance when compelled to do so either because they have suffered an injustice or by popular demand. State envoys may come and go unhindered, are received with ceremony, and usually seen off with gifts for the people and their ruler. If an envoy is in any way grieved or wronged, it is a grave affront and severe reprisals are taken. When the envoys are unwelcome, they encounter a somber mien, and in the absence of a desire to negotiate, the gifts that are normally presented beforehand are not accepted. This shows them that they had better leave sooner than later and, moreover, their lives may be in danger. Were any harm to befall the envoys, the only redress is strict retaliation. It may be that their nation is already engaged in other wars or does not feel itself strong enough, in which case they may defer taking action in order to seek help or gain an advantage later, but they will never forget it.

Of Gifts and Offerings

All their treaties, accords, peace negotiations, atonements, proposals, requests, contracts, and pledges are sealed and sanctioned with gifts and offerings. Without these, their acts and promises are not worth much, but when followed or preceded by a presentation, they are regarded as duly executed and attested. That is why an offering is commonly made with each point requested or agreed, the points being represented and remembered by means of wooden tallies that they have with them for that purpose. While each subject, article, or point is being stipulated, determined, and recapitulated, the person making the request or speech has the offering either before him or in his hand. At the close of the parley he places it before the one for whom it is intended. Matters thus concluded with and among them they will exactly remember and perform to the utmost by all possible means. The offerings they make usually consist of *sewant*, pelts, duffel cloth, and munitions of war, very seldom of grains.

They are ever ready to exchange gifts among themselves and also with our nation, who are not keen on it, however, because the Indians tend to demand too much in return and appropriate what the other party does not give of his own accord. When making a request to one of them or in general, one sends an offering to the respective person or locality. The offering is hung up, the request is stated, and those to whom it is addressed examine and deliberate the proposition seriously. If they take the offering, the request as made is accepted and consented to, but if it remains where it hangs for over three days, the matter is held in abeyance and the petitioner has to alter the conditions or augment the offering or both.

Of the Indians' Government and Public Policy

Public policy in the proper sense does not exist, but there is a glimmer of government and something that in broad terms suggests policy. Government is of the popular kind, so much so that it is in many respects defective and lame. It consists of the chiefs, the nobles, and the tribal and family elders. Only when military matters are being considered are the war chiefs consulted as well. Those together constitute all there is of council, governance, and rule.

They consider everything at great length and spare no time when the matter is of any importance. No particular order of seating is observed, though when traveling, rank is to some extent recognized in that the worthiest of them walks in front. In case of equal claims, the oldest or the one who is on home ground has precedence, but without noticeable ceremony or compliment. When a matter has been decided in the aforesaid manner, the populace is summoned to the chief's house or wherever the council has met. A person gifted with eloquence and a strong, penetrating voice is called upon to speak. He recounts in the fullest detail, in a formal address and as agreeably as he can, what was deliberated, decided, and resolved. Then there is silence all around, and meanwhile, the chiefs try to gain the community's approval of the decisions. If they encounter difficulties, they have various means of securing acceptance, for the commonalty normally has to carry out what has been decided, and without its consent they cannot make much progress. Therefore each of them recommends the matter very particularly and earnestly to the family in which he is foremost. It may happen occasionally during the assembly that the chiefs face impertinent and unseemly behavior by a suspicious, unruly, and biased person. Then one of the younger chiefs will jump up and in one fell swoop smash the man's skull with an ax in full view of everyone. No one will intervene or become involved beyond carrying off and burying the body. This happens but seldom and never without persuasion having been tried first.[37] Yet I have been told by prominent Indians that sometimes a resolution adopted by such means, and having only the appearance of upholding the rights of council members, is approved, praised, and loudly acclaimed, after which it has great force and rarely fails to be given effect.

Their Religion and Whether They Can Be Christianized

They are all heathens, have no particular religion or devotion, and no known idols or images they venerate, let alone worship. When swearing an oath, they take as witness the sun, regarded as all-seeing. They have great affection for the moon, as governing all growth, yet do not worship or pay homage to it. The other planets and stars they know by name, and through that knowledge and from other signs they are fairly weather wise.

To pray and celebrate holy days or anything like it is not known among them. They do know something of God, as we shall remark later, and are in great fear of the devil, for he harms and torments them. When they have been out fishing or hunting, they customarily throw a portion of the catch into the fire without ceremony and say, "There, devil, you eat that."

They appreciate hearing about God and our religion, and during our services and prayers they keep very quiet and seem to pay attention, but in reality they have no notion of these matters. They live without religion and inner or outward devotion; even superstition and idolatry are unknown to them, and they follow the dictates of nature alone. For that reason some suppose that they may all the easier be led to the knowledge and fear of God. Among some nations the word for Sunday is known, which they call Kintowen.[38] The oldest among them say that in early times a greater knowledge and fear of God existed and add, "Because we are unable to read and write, and the people are becoming more wicked, the Sunday has fallen into disuse and oblivion." When [one is] talking earnestly with them about this, they show some signs of regret, but none of emotion. When one berates them, individually or generally, for some wicked act or speech on the ground that it incurs the wrath of God in heaven, they reply, "We do not know that God or where he is and have never seen him; if you know and fear him, as you say you do, how come there are so many whores, thieves, drunkards, and other evildoers among you; surely that God of yours will punish you severely, since he warned you of it. He never warned us and left us in ignorance; therefore we do not deserve punishment."[39]

Very seldom do they adopt our religion, nor have any particular official measures been resorted to or applied to induce them to do so. When their children are still young, it happens that our people take them into the home as servants and as opportunities arise give them some slight religious instruction, but when they grow to be young men and women and begin to mix with the other Indians, they soon forget what they never learned thoroughly and revert to Indian ways and manners. The Jesuits in Canada have made an effort and led many to the Roman Catholic religion, but because they have no inner inclination toward it, or were not properly taught the principles and have regard to appearances only, they easily lapse from the faith and actually mock it. Thus it happened when a certain merchant, who still resides among us, went up to trade with the Indians in the year 1639 and got into a discussion on religion with a chief who spoke French well, which the merchant also understood very well. After they had downed five or six glasses of wine, the chief said, "I myself had so far been instructed in religion by your people that I frequently said mass among the Indians. Once upon a time the place in which the altar stood accidentally caught fire, and the people rushed forward to quench it, but I checked them, saying the God standing there is almighty and will shortly make the fire go out by itself. Then we waited expectantly, but the fire burned steadily on until it had consumed everything, including even your almighty God and all the fine objects around him. Ever since I have disliked religion and esteemed the sun and the moon much more and better than all your gods, for they [the sun and the moon] warm the earth and make the crops grow, and your God cannot save himself from fire."

In all that country I know no more than just one person [among the Indians] who is an ornament to religion. Nor is it to be expected, as long as the matter is thus suffered to drag on, that many Indians will through instruction be led to religion. Public authority ought to become involved and provide for sound teaching of our language and the elements of the Christian religion to their youth in good schools, established in suitable locations in that country, so that in due course they could and would teach each other further and take pleasure in doing so. It would take a deal of effort and preparation, but without such measures not much good can be achieved among them. The neglect of it is a very bad thing, since the Indians themselves say they would be happy to have their children instructed in our language and religion.[40]

Of Their Sentiments regarding Hope of Afterlife

It is cause for great wonder and strong evidence against all unbelieving freethinkers that these people who are so barbaric and wild, as has been shown, nevertheless are able to distinguish between body and soul, and believe, as in fact they do, the one to be perishable and the other immortal. The soul, they say, is that which animates and rules the body and from which spring all the virtues and vices. When separated from the body at death, the soul travels to a region to the southward so equable one never needs protective covering against the cold, yet not so hot as to be uncomfortable.[41] That is the destination of the souls who were good and virtuous in this life, and where they enjoy everything in abundance, for all things needed are in infinite supply without requiring any labor. Those who in this life were wicked and evil will be in another place differing completely in condition and qualities from the first, nor will they enjoy anything like the contentment of the virtuous. Whether the body will at some time be reunited with the soul I have never been able to ascertain from them. I have spoken with Christians who thought to have heard them say so, but I cannot confirm it.

When they hear voices or sounds coming from the woods in the dead of night that we reckon were made by a wild animal, they say in amazement, "What you hear calling there are the souls of wicked persons who are doomed to wander about and haunt the woods and wilderness in the night and at unseasonable times." For fear of them the Indians will not go anywhere at night, unless in a group when they must; otherwise they take a torch. They are frightened of evil spirits who, they believe, remain intent on hurting and terrifying them. They confess and believe also that the soul comes from, and is given by, God.

That is what one may on occasion learn from them when

talking in a serious vein with the old and wise; more could probably be gotten from them if one knew their language thoroughly. Among the common people or the youngsters, one never hears those matters spoken of, but one can nevertheless see the righteousness of God, who through the universal light of mankind's nature has made these people understand, recognize, and surmise that the reward for doing good and evil awaits men after this life.

79   Of the Knowledge of God and the Fear of Devils

Although the original natives of New Netherland are heathens and unbelievers, they all know and confess that there is a God in heaven, eternal and almighty. Since God is in the highest degree good and merciful, they aver, and unwilling to hurt or punish any human being, he does not concern himself at all with the ordinary affairs of the world. The devil takes advantage of the scope thus given him, and all that happens to man here below, they believe the devil disposes, guides, and governs at will. God, or the chief superior who dwells in heaven, is no doubt much greater and higher than the devil and also has dominion over him, but declines to become involved in all those troubles.

When we respond to this by saying that the devil is evil, cunning, and wicked, they frankly admit that to be true and also that he takes great pleasure in directing all matters in as baneful a way as he can. They further maintain that every misfortune, scourge, calamity, and infirmity is inflicted on them by the devil. They express with the general appellation of devil, all accidents and illnesses they suffer. For example, in case of an internal disorder they say there is a devil within my body, and if something ails them in an arm, leg, foot, hand, shoulder, or the head they say, pointing to the affected part, there is a devil inside. Since the devil is so malicious and merciless toward them, they have no choice but to fear and yet keep on friendly terms with him, and sometimes throw a morsel into the fire to please him, as stated above.[42]

When we refute these absurdities easily, we do so by telling them that God is omniscient and omnipotent; knows the nature of devils exactly; quietly observes their doings; and will not permit a puffed-up and faithless servant to tyrannize man, who is the most glorious creature of all and made in God's image, provided he duly puts his trust in God and does not forsake his commandments in favor of evil. To that they respond with an odd and fantastic argument: "You Dutch say so, and seen superficially it may seem to be as you maintain, but you do not understand the matter aright. This God, who is supremely good, almighty, and beneficent, Lord of heaven and earth and all its host, is not alone up there in heaven without any company or diversion, but has with him a goddess or a woman who is the fairest the eye has ever beheld or can behold. With this goddess or beauty he passes and forgets the time, being deeply attached to her, and meanwhile the devil plays the lord on earth and does whatever he wishes." That conviction is firmly inculcated in them, and no matter how far one pursues the argument and reasons with them, whatever abominable absurdities they resort to, and whether one checkmates them in debate, in the end they return to the view, like a dog that licks up its own vomit, that the devil must be served because he has power to harm them.

80

Their Thoughts on the Creation and Propagation of Mankind and Animals in the World

From Indian youths or those met with among our people and still partly in a state of nature, no certainty or reply concerning this subject is to be had. One must await a suitable opportunity to raise it with more mature and wiser persons if he is to get some indication of it. It may happen in the course of a serious discussion that they themselves inquire after our views on the origin of mankind. When we then relate the creation of Adam, in broken language and to the best of our ability, they cannot or will not understand it in regard to their own nation or the Negroes, on account of the difference in skin color. As they see it, the world was not created the way we believe it was and as told in Genesis 1 and 2. They say that before the world and the mountains, humans, and animals came into existence, God was with the woman who dwells with him, and no one knows when that was or where they had come from. Water was all there was, or at any rate water covered and overran everything. Even if an eye had existed at that time, it could not have seen anything but water wherever it might have been, for all was water or was covered by water. What then took place, they say, was that the aforementioned beautiful woman or idol descended from heaven into the water. She was gross and big like a woman who is pregnant with more than one child. Touching down gently, she did not sink deep, for at once a patch of land began to emerge under her at the spot where she had come down, and there she came to rest and remained. The land waxed greater so that dry patches became visible around the place where she sat, as happens to someone standing on a sandbar in three or four feet of water while it ebbs away and eventually recedes so far that it leaves him entirely on dry land. That is how it went with the descended goddess, they say and believe, the land ever widening around her until its edge disappeared from view. Gradually grass and other vegetation sprang up and in time, also fruit-bearing and other trees, and from this, in brief, the whole globe came into being much as it appears to this day. Now, whether the world you speak of and originally came from was then created as well, we are unable to say.

At the time when all that had been brought about, the high

personage went into labor and, being confined, gave birth to three different creatures. The first was in every respect like a deer as they are today, the second resembled a bear, and the third a wolf. The woman suckled these creatures until maturity and remained on earth for a considerable time, during which she cohabited with each of the said animals and was delivered a number of times of various creatures in multiple births. Thus were bred all humans and animals of the several kinds and species that are still to be seen in our day. In due course, they began to segregate according to the genera and species still existing, both from an innate urge and for the sake of propriety. When all those things had thus been disposed and made self-perpetuating, the universal mother ascended again to heaven, rejoicing at having accomplished her task. There she continues to dwell forever, finding her entire happiness and delight in keeping and fostering the supreme Lord's love for her. To that she is devoted, and from it derives her complete enjoyment and satisfaction; therefore, God vouchsafes her his fondest love and highest esteem.[43]

Here below, meanwhile, humans and animals of all the various species that were the result of miscegenation increase and multiply, as does all creation the way we find it still. That is why human beings of whatever condition still exhibit the innate characters of one or other of the three animals mentioned, for they are either timid and harmless in the nature of deer, or vindictive, cruel, bold, and direct in the nature of bears, or bloodthirsty, greedy, cunning, and treacherous like wolves. That all this has changed somewhat now and is no longer clearly visible or recognized, they attribute to the times and people's guile in disguising it. This, they say, is all we have heard on the subject from our ancestors and believe to be true. Had they been able to write like ourselves, they might have left us a more complete account, but they could not. There you have, dear reader, all that I have been able to ascertain and that was worth writing down generally and in detail concerning the folkways of the Indians of New Netherland, including most of what from the beginning individual Christians over there have come to know. Even where it is fantastic and contrary to truth, I thought fit to put it simply before you in writing. The wise, as I have heard them philosophize, think and speculate deeply about it and, as the saying goes, know like Virgil how to distill gold from Ennius's dung.[44]

OF THE NATURE, AMAZING WAYS, AND PROPERTIES OF THE BEAVERS

Under the heading of wildlife in the description of the animals of New Netherland, we left it until later to relate in detail the nature and unusual habits of the beavers. Since we have said as much as we deem necessary of the country and its natives, now is the time to keep our promise. As the beaver is the main reason and the source of the means for the initial settlement of this fine country by Europeans, it will be appropriate to go some way back regarding its nature and attributes and first to record the views that ancient and later authors expressed about the animal. It will then appear from the subsequent account of the plain and simple truth how far all of them strayed from the facts.

The great naturalist Pliny, in the third chapter of his thirty-second book, states that the beaver's members, by which he means the testes, have many medicinal uses, and that the beavers, knowing that trappers pursue them for that reason, bite off those parts with their teeth, and as a last resort, rise up and show them to the trappers so that they may be rid of the prize they are hunted for.[1] All the ancient naturalists and physicians were of that opinion. Later this was denied by some who, nevertheless, believed that beavers were caught merely for their genitals, which they called castoreum, or beaver testes. They also write that beavers have sharp teeth with which they can fell trees as though cut down with an ax. Olaus and Albertus mention the beavers' carrying of wood and their nest building.[2] All of them thought that beavers had long and fishlike tails, that they bit people fiercely if they could reach them, and more of such things, some of which had a semblance of truth and others none at all. From this it may be inferred and believed that none of them had ever seen a beaver but depended on the loose talk of ordinary inexperienced persons, which is unreliable. It is quite another matter and more deserving of credit when they speak of the singular medicinal effects of beaver flesh and members. That was their field and that they knew from experience; the rest they took on faith, even though it was told by those who also did not know. Therefore, and since it is to the point, we insert here a summary of what they considered to be the medicinal properties of the beaver.

Smelling beaver glands makes people sneeze. Castoreum mixed with rose oil and drippings from lard, rubbed on the temples or taken with water, restores sleep; therefore, it is also useful in treating lunatics. Touching a sleeping person with beaver glands awakens him. Two drams of castoreum taken with mint water brings on the menses in women and expels the afterbirth. Castoreum rubbed on [the body] is good for dizziness, trembling, gout, paralysis, stomach ache, and palpitation; also, when taken internally, it cures epilepsy, constipation, bellyache, and poisoning. Against toothache, crushed beaver gland mixed with oil is to be dripped into the ear on the side that hurts, and against ringing in the ears the mixture is dripped into the ears through muslin cloth. When mixed with the best honey and rubbed on the eyes, castoreum promotes sharp and clear vision. Beaver urine is effective against various poisons; it will keep well if stored in the beaver's bladder. Sufferers from podagra should make boots and shoes of beaver skin and wear them daily.[3]

Having stated the above by way of introduction, we shall now truthfully present the real nature of the beaver as we personally have found it to be and have been informed by unimpeachable witnesses. And that none may think that we, too, treat of a matter unknown to us, we beg the reader to note that in New Netherland and adjacent districts, some eighty-thousand beavers are put down every year, that we, during the nine years we were there, often made a meal of beaver meat, also kept them from a young age, and handled many thousands of beaver skins.

The beaver is a four-legged animal that feeds on plants, lives in water and on land, has a fine and thick coat, is low on its legs, quick, timid, clever, and about as broad as it is long. It is called *castor* in Greek, *fiber* in Latin, and *beever* in Dutch, and most of the other names by which it is known in Europe are derived from the above.[4] Its four legs resemble those of the otter or other wild and domestic animals living on land only. Its food is not fish or prey, like the otter's, as is supposed by some who accordingly depict and describe the beaver with a fish in its mouth or even as being part fish, part flesh; they eat the bark of various trees and roots, grass, rushes, and greens growing on the watersides and in the bushes and fields thereabouts. The bark is mostly that of willows, osiers, and aspen growing by the waterside.[5] Failing that, [beavers eat] various other plants that are free of the sour or bitter taste they cannot bear. Beavers live, as is said and is true, both in water and on land and may therefore be called semiaquatic, though in the main they keep to dry land. They get most of their food on land—the tree bark and small plants they eat—as well as the wood and grass for building their lodges and spend entire nights on land. Nor can they stay underwater for long, particularly when they are being hunted and get tired. Underwater they find for their sustenance little more than the bark of some roots that protrude from the banks of running streams and rushes growing here and there, mostly at the water's edge. That beavers are so often in the water is surely because, as attested by all the big beaver trappers, they are by nature timid and reckon they are more secure and better able to save themselves in water than on land. Therefore, as will be told later, they have their lodges in the water, and these have openings in the lower part through which they can go by water to a retreat that they always have nearby: a cave or burrow underwater in the side of the stream in which their dwelling is situated. Into this they retire and stay in time of need, feeling that inside they are so well protected that no one can harm them.

The beaver pelt, or skin, is thick and is densely covered all over with very fine fur. The color is ash gray tending toward pale blue, and the tips may be brownish or russet. The fur is made into the best hats that are worn, named beavers or castors for the material they are made of and by now well known throughout Europe. On top of the fur some shiny hair is to be seen, which is known as guard hair or more properly winter hair, since it falls out in summer and regrows in autumn. This hair is normally chestnut brown, and the browner the better; it may also have a reddish tint. For hat making it is pulled out, being coarse and of no value. If the skins are first to go from here to Muscovy, however, as is usual and happens regularly, the shiny hair is what makes them sought after. It seems that the Muscovites value the skins for this hair and cut them into strips and edging for women's overcoats, as is done here with rabbit and similar skins. They also dress the skins, hence known as pelts. That person among them who owns the most and the best ranks as the grandest, like someone here who is decked out in fine cloth and gold and silver.

By the time the guard hair has gone and the skins are old, soiled, and seemingly worn out, they are returned to be made into hats. Before then, the skins are unsuitable for that purpose, for unless beaver fur is dirty, soiled, and greasy, it will not felt. Therefore, the worn pelts are much in demand. Coats made by the Indians of beaver skin, worn on the bare body for a time, and made dirty from sweat and greasiness, work well and yield good hats. Those skins, before being sent to Muscovy, are also used to obtain beaver hair known as combings, because it is removed with a comb from under the guard hair. This then is blended with the [remaining] fur received back from Muscovy, to facilitate further processing.

Beavers have very short and, so to speak, no legs or shanks. When they walk, one can see hardly any semblance or shape of legs on them; they seem to move on no more than small paws that are closely attached to the body. The claws or paws are hairless, blackish in color, and have strong brown nails at the toes, which are joined by thick skin, thus resembling swans' feet, though not as broad. The forepaws are shorter and narrower than the hind paws. The hindquarter is short and much like that of a swan or a goose. As the animal has a very short or practically no neck, and the head is set close to the shoulders, its forepaws are quite near the head, so that when walking, which beavers can nevertheless do with singular quickness, the whole of the heavy, thickset body touches the ground and seems to overwhelm the short little legs. Far from it, though; beavers are very alert, well endowed with sinews and muscles, and, therefore, tremendously strong. They are agile and can run amazingly fast, considering their shape, when escaping from dogs and people. In water as well, they can rapidly get to where they want to be as if they were actually fish. Therefore, the Indians have to catch them in traps or, when the beavers lie concealed in their burrows underground, lance them with long rapier blades mounted on shafts.

That beavers, according to Olaus Magnus and Albertus, are prone to bite people severely is a misapprehension, for they are timid animals that will try to save themselves by fleeing, if at all possible, and not by violence. As they have, also, a keen sense of smell and sharp hearing, one seldom gets to see them in the wild. Nor will they ever go where people are about, as many otters may do, but instead keep to dense bush near water and wetlands, away from human beings. When set upon and bitten by dogs, however, they defend themselves fiercely and can put an average dog out of action if they get hold of it with their front teeth. As to beavers biting people so savagely, I have seen and spoken with hundreds of beaver trappers, but never to my knowledge with more than one who had by accident been injured rather badly in his shoulder by a cornered beaver when he went to help his dog, which was mixed up with it and struggling, and the beaver, perhaps to its own amazement, happened to bite the dog's master instead of the dog.

That beavers are clever is shown by the building of their dwellings and the rearing of their young, which we shall describe presently, as well as by the continual watch they keep to avoid being surprised and caught. I am told that they keep watch, and take regular turns at doing so, at every lodge, which usually houses a family of six or seven or more living together. It is a fact that when it is freezing hard, as it often does where the most and the best beavers live, one of them will always be sitting close to running water—for I have never heard or known that they build anywhere but near running water—to keep it open by slapping its tail on the water's surface. They do not always sit halfway in the water, as Olaus Magnus and Albertus thought, for the hard frost makes that impossible, and in any case beavers can be out of the water without discomfort—contrary to the above views. This [the tail-slapping] one may picture as though someone continuously slapped the water with the flat of his hand and fingers to keep it from freezing over. They do this, not because beavers cannot endure being out of the water, according to the [animal] doctors, but in order to keep the entrances [of their lodges] open, so that they can come out and forage, and also, when pursued, seek refuge easily and at little risk in the stronghold they have close-by under the riverbank.

The shape of the beaver suggests a cucumber with a flat stalk at one end, or is like a duck minus the neck and the head, or like an elongated and somewhat flat ball of yarn that may also be thicker than it is long. Like a hog, whose sides run fairly straight from the back to the belly, the beaver resembles a dead mole that has been trod on but not entirely flattened. The pelt of an adult beaver is reckoned [in the trade] at one ell across, that is to say one ell long and as wide, when not round, but approximately square, as is normal. Bigger than that is accepted as good merchantable, up to five quarters [of an ell], and they are rarely more. In winter, from December to May and into June, the pelts are good, and that is also when most beavers are killed. The autumn pelts do have some guard hair but have little fur underneath it. The summer pelts and the pelts of beavers killed before they are fully grown are not worth much. The Indians do not spare them, however, and take all they come across or can get hold of when on the hunt.

The beavers build their homes, as Sextus, Albertus, and Olaus correctly note, of wood and always in running water, with several stories, up to four, five, and more, on top of one another, so ingenious and curious that it is impressive and striking to see owing to all those compartments and levels.[6] They close up the top with clay, wood, and grass tightly enough to keep out most of the rain. There they live, all or part of a generation together, and break away like bees accordingly after multiplying and if left relatively undisturbed. The wood of which they build their lodges is soft, such as aspen, pine, tulip tree, or the like that they find lying about near the water's edge. This they use first, and when it runs out they go to the nearest forest and fell trees in the following manner. A beaver wishing to cut down a tree selects one of about a foot and a half around and whose bark is not bad tasting to it. It then starts gnawing at the tree with its front incisors. In the front of the mouth beavers have two upper and two lower teeth of great strength that extend about half an inch from the gums or less or more depending on its age. The teeth are yellowish on the surface, and this material, when removed by scorching and ingested, is thought to be a sovereign remedy for jaundice. Like the teeth of squirrels, weasels, minks, and mice of this country, these are set in the forward part of the mouth. The beaver gnaws a groove a hand's breadth or six inches wide, depending on the girth of the tree, works right around and up and down until the cut reaches the center and goes through it, and the tree falls. The two sides of the cut look as though turned in the shape of big tops—such as children spin with a whip—set against each other with the points touching. Whether the beaver looks up when the tree is about to fall I have been unable to learn, but it often happens that a tree has been gnawed through and slips off the stump without falling, because it leans against the other trees around it and so remains upright. I and others with me have seen many such trees in the forest. As regards moving the wood to the building site, all who live in New Netherland often see pelts whose guard hair on the back is worn off, and they call those wood carriers, because the pelts [belonged to beavers that] carried wood when they ran short during building. They do not carry the wood between their legs [and drag it] like a sled or cart, as the ancients thought they did; Indians who declared that they had seen it have told me that the beavers cut sections [of the tree trunk] with their teeth to the length and weight of the one that is to carry it, then the female places herself underneath, and the kits and the male guide and support [the piece of wood] lest it fall off, and so it goes until they have enough. That they let themselves be dragged by the tail while they hold the wood against the body is devoid of truth, for their tails are not, as the ancients believed, big and long; the very biggest are not stouter than an average man's hand without the thumb, as well as too tender to stand the force of being dragged, particularly when held by such sharp teeth.[7]

Beaver tails are flattish and hairless and have the appearance of being set with fish scales, but it is actually the skin that is so grained. The tail, like all of the beaver, is a delicate food, and that is why in Germany beavers are always reserved for the emperor's table on the rare occasions they are caught. The meat excels all other meat of land or water animals. Hence the Indians, who for little recompense gladly share their foodstuffs and meals with us, seldom part with beaver meat, so that most of the Christians of New Netherland have never tasted it. And the very finest and best part of all the beaver is the tail, which the Indians will not lightly give up, other than as an exceptional treat or gift for someone.

Beavers, like hogs, have a gestation period of sixteen weeks and see to it that they litter once a year during summer, some earlier than others. They always give birth to four young at a time, unless it is the first litter, when only two or three may be born. As soon as the young beavers come into the world, they cry like newborn children, so that a person coming to where there is a young beaver, and not being forewarned, may think that a small child is near. Between their forepaws, which are set close to the head, but far enough apart, the beaver has two teats as women have. When the kits want to suck, they come up two at a time, for there are no more teats than that.[8] The mother then raises herself like a human being sitting up and gives a teat to each of the kits, who lean against the mother's body like children who stand and suck. Meanwhile, the others lie in the nest as though they lay crying, and so they carry on in turns.

A young beaver is a gentle creature and can be easily kept,

88

reared, and domesticated like a dog. Like cats they then eat everything, but no fish or meat, but if it is first boiled for them they will get used to it. When quite young they need to be fed on milk, which they quickly learn to suck through a strip of cloth or a horn. They can be made as docile as a pup and never bite or get cross, however much one teases them. As they grow a little older, the young beavers like to get down to the water for a wash every day, and there they tumble and play in the stream. They are so playful and lively that it is a pleasure to watch them. The pity is that, because people over there do not usually fence their farms along the water, the daily coming and going soon leads the beavers into the open country, and they think no more of returning, like deer and other animals that can likewise be kept and made quite tame.

Physicians attribute special qualities to beaver glands, named castoreum by them, as mentioned earlier. Aristotle, Pliny, and others of their time thought that the beavers themselves bit off those glands, but Olaus Magnus, Agricola, Albertus, and Sextus were not prepared to accept this and added that deception often attended the sale of beaver glands, as is indeed true.[9] I have taken great pains to come to a correct understanding of the matter; to that end I not only closely questioned many Indians whom I considered to be the most experienced, but also with my own hands opened up and carefully examined several beavers. Therefore, I shall not at this point keep it from the indulgent reader how I fared.

The position is that beaver glands for medicinal purposes used to come from Canada, dried and in kegs, and also, I was told, salted for sale to druggists; but because the greater part consisted of beaver kidneys, nipples, or other than the right glands, they later fell out of favor. Several people sailed from New Netherland with what they believed was a good amount of beaver glands—and the Indians from whom they obtained them knew no better—but on arrival in Holland, they could not do much with it and were told that these were not the right kind. Hearing of this more than once, I became curious and began to doubt whether what I had seen actually were true beaver glands. Those I had seen were round and of varying size, and always dripped grease, like lard melting in the sun, no matter how long they were hung to smoke or dry. Eventually I saw one of an elongated shape like a candied pear, wrinkled and somewhat mucous, and this I showed to an experienced physician resident in New Netherland. I understood from him that this was of the right kind and as they ought to be. At about that time, when beavers were living not very far from my home, Indian trappers brought me several that had not yet been cut up and were whole and quite fresh. I made an effort to find out where and how the true beaver glands were situated, but it was in vain. I found nothing but little round balls deep inside the carcass under the pubic bone and the thighbones, like the ordinary type that was said in Holland not to be the right sort. At long last, and after I had told a knowledgeable Indian about this and shown him some of the best kind of gland shaped like a pear, I took his advice, as he was a great beaver trapper well known to me and who assisted me in all this business: I operated on a female beaver that was big with young, as I was also keen to see those and how they lay. Thus I found, up against the spine, two glands of the shape I sought, yellowish, oblong like a pear, but flatter, of a substance similar to calf sweetbread and coated with a rather tough membrane. I took them out, and to make doubly sure they were from a female, also removed four kits from the same carcass. Some time later I showed these beaver glands to the aforementioned doctor of medicine at the governor's house amid full company and asked those present what they thought these were. The doctor and all the others judged them to be the true beaver glands. When I told them the whole story they looked surprised but stuck to their first opinion that these were true beaver glands.[10]

On later occasions I cut open more beavers and always fared as here related, so that in my opinion, without wishing to prejudge anyone else's views, the real castoreum is to be found in the females, and not in the males. The little round balls taken from the males the Indians carve up and smoke with tobacco, which they say is wholesome and tasty.[11]

The Indians relish beaver flesh and the fat around the body, of as much as two or three fingers thick, and are particularly fond of the tail and the flesh layered between fatty tissue in the lard, as in fattened hogs. But beaver bones they burn and will not let their dogs eat, lest the latter become unlucky in the hunt, as they believe.

Beavers are all of the same color, with some a little browner and others a little redder. Once only have I seen a snow white beaver, and as far as can be ascertained, the same is true of all who have ever handled beavers. That one, whose guard hair on the back had a slight golden gleam, was lost at sea with Director Kieft in the ship *Princess*.

A CONVERSATION BETWEEN A DUTCH PATRIOT AND A NEW NETHERLANDER CONCERNING THE CONDITION OF NEW NETHERLAND

PATRIOT: Sir and friend, I have before now duly read and been told of the natural features of New Netherland, the appearance and ways of its aborigines, and related matters, by which I am satisfied that, then as now, a citizen, farmer, or other private person of whatever condition can do well for himself there. Yet some queries have occurred to me, to which I have long wished to hear your response. Allow me, therefore, to state my concerns by way of questions, the easier to achieve my objective.

The first is whether it would be advantageous to this nation that the said country should prosper, and what would be the benefit that this nation could gain by it.

Second, even if the country's population and wealth were to increase, is its situation such that it can be defended, or, could be made so, against attack by enemies and pirates?

And third, whether it offers good opportunities for business, in which places, and in what goods one could with advantage trade from there. My further queries, to be brief, can be inferred from the above or are implied by them. On all this I am keen to be enlightened by you, if you will.

NEW NETHERLANDER: Though I, dear sir, am not as well qualified as I could wish to answer those farseeing questions, I shall, since you wish it, attempt to satisfy you.

First, then, whether it serves the interests of this nation that New Netherland prosper. To that I say yes, for these reasons or, to answer you more nearly, the advantages that can thus accrue to this nation consist of the following. First, if troubles arose with Spain, which God forbid, then no place on earth would be better suited than this one to strike at her heart and vitals. There everything is available, because provisions and wood such as planks, props, masts, and whatever is needed for outfitting ships, either are in ample supply or can be had if an effort were made, without involving anyone but ourselves.

Second, if by some mischance we were to suffer a shortage of iron, wood, ashes [potash], wheat, or anything obtained from Baltic shores, the New Netherlanders need only arrange matters accordingly and the shortfall could be made good from there, provided we first saw to an increase in the population, for all comes to naught if that is lacking.

Third, many will ever find a free and untroubled refuge there and conduct free and profitable trade both ways between these two domains of the States General. With the passage of time trade will increase and develop so much that any estimate made of it now will seem suspect. One can see how trade has expanded in the past two or three years since a beginning was made with peopling the country, and if this is continued, trade will grow incredibly from year to year, but more of this when we come to your third question.

Fourth, in times of emergency this state could procure from there, as the population increases, formidable assistance and supplies of men and provisions, such as makes a republic respected and esteemed by all who might be envious of its prosperity.

And fifth, it is well known that normally a great many

persons migrate to this country since they have never been unwanted and always used to find employment, but now, in time of peace and for other reasons, not so much employment is offered here and many, as it were, walk the streets without means of support. It surely follows that it would be useful and quite feasible to establish, with the aid of those dispensable and redundant folk, another Netherland outside the Netherlands as a notable sheet anchor and support of the state. With that I consider your first question answered.

PATRIOT: In general terms I can see reason in what you are saying, but I have often heard respectable persons declare that Spain herself is hardly thankful for having so 92 many overseas colonies, because they attract such numbers of people that it frequently causes difficulties at home and leaves good positions vacant and promising opportunities unused. One knows, of course, that first things come first, and the shirt goes on before the coat; what is your view on that?

NEW NETHERLANDER: As regards Spain, it is evident that without her overseas colonies she would not be nearly as powerful as she is; that is obvious. It may well be true that her colonies draw away and absorb very many people, and as a result some of the minor posts in Spain remain vacant, but between the situation of Spain and that of these United Netherlands, the difference in that respect is so great that all the arguments against it in their case turn out to be arguments in favor in ours. It would be tiresome to go into this at length, but stated briefly, Spain is surrounded by countries such as Italy, France, and Portugal, where, as in Spain herself, alert local people find plentiful employment while, more so than in this country, death and warfare exact a heavy toll. From our neighboring countries, however, from eastern Europe, Germany, Westphalia, Scandinavia,

Wallonia, etc., a host of people arrive in the Netherlands. Despite the many job opportunities, a good few thousand annually could still be dispensed with and sent across—and indeed ought to be, for otherwise the flow would cease and the country's reputation in this respect suffer—since any shortage that might arise could again be met from outside. In short, we can use those folk and turn them into Hollanders, while our neighbors must rear them for us. Those going to New Netherland are not lost or wasted, but in a sense, [are] put out at interest in view of the natural increase taking place there.

PATRIOT: Are you implying that the Netherlands is a better country than eastern Europe, Germany, etc.?

NEW NETHERLANDER: That is not the impression we mean to give; we feel that if the question were to arise it would answer itself, but it cannot be denied that in the provinces of this state there are now, by the grace of God, more commercial houses, factories, cash resources, indeed business activity and prosperity than in any of the countries mentioned, although some of the Hanseatic cities are not to be ignored either. And where there is carrion gather the eagles. Also, the Dutch have compassionate natures and regard foreigners virtually as native citizens, which is an attraction, the more so when, in addition, everyone of whatever trade he may be and who is prepared to adapt, can always get off to a good start here. In the course of time this has become the customary practice.

On the basis of all of which, I conclude that out of this country we could found as many colonies as Spain possesses, even half as many again, without missing a single Hollander or anyone from the Netherlands. We should actually gain people, because those living in New Netherland or similar colonies turn into Hollanders as effectively as those from abroad who become citizens here and always remain loyal to us.

93

PATRIOT: Now I am beginning to follow you in this, that settlement over there would not be unrewarding to this nation, but there is something else: Suppose persons of standing and means went across, as I hear now occasionally happens, or, since it is reported that good business can be done, that diligent or fortunate persons were to prosper there, for then they also become people of standing, or at least their descendants will be; what security for their persons and possessions can they have?—certainly not all the time, I expect.

NEW NETHERLANDER: Excuse me, sir, but now you do me an injustice, for that is actually the second question on which you indicated a desire to hear me, and here you pass a hasty and ill-considered judgment on it.

PATRIOT: Not so ill-considered as you may think, for I am mindful that the country was simply found by us and easily acquired, that it lies open to seaward and landward and is equipped with only a few forts, and those of little consequence. Also, that the English and the Indians all around are strong, and we weak, and that the Portuguese or other pirates would have no trouble invading the country from the sea, and in short order too, for it is within easy reach and not far from the sea lanes. What is more, you well know that our people, especially those who are business oriented—and I can understand that business must be a priority there—are quick to do some buying and selling, but take little care to secure or fortify a territory unless they are military men, who are few out there. All in all, I see a big problem, for one cannot be secure in the possession of what he may have brought over or gained and saved there.

NEW NETHERLANDER: If you are inclined to supply your own answers or prejudge matters, I may as well be silent, for even if I demonstrated the contrary it would make no difference. Your arguments have a superficial appearance of reason and truth but are so indiscriminate and confused that they seem to mean something and actually amount to nothing.

PATRIOT: Then I shall gladly await your intimations and promise to listen without prejudice or bias, for otherwise this would be, as you say, a futile exercise.

NEW NETHERLANDER: You are right to do so; it is the only way to get to the truth of the matter. Therefore I shall go over all your objections so far as my memory serves me.

What the country is like and how we acquired it can be read in the description given of it, so it would be superfluous to relate that here. Of the country having been easily come by, little need be said, as this is true only of the initial discovery. But considering the costs incurred at the time by individuals and then by the West India Company and others, together amounting to many tons of gold, along with the efforts made and precautions taken from time to time, we did not acquire it easily, that is to say, we did not get to where we are now without much cost, difficulty, and trouble.

When you say, as your second point, that the country lies open by water and by land and is poorly equipped with forts, you again go too far and exaggerate, for mark this: Both the South River and the North River are pilot waters and impossible to enter without grave danger by those who are unfamiliar with the situation. Furthermore, the sandbars and flats frequently shift their positions. Assuming the enemy managed to enter, that would not be all, for they would then have to reach places where they could do something and pass forts that, relative to local conditions, are as substantial as any in this country. And if with increase in population and means, as you rightly observe, the need became greater, the land fortifies itself remarkably and also lends itself naturally to fortification at Sandy Hook, The Narrows, Hell Gate, or at other bays and entrances so as to make it, humanly speaking, impregnable. Until we reach the stage of having a few [fortifications], we run little risk, for in snatching a penny from someone, nobody likes to lose two.

PATRIOT: That is all well and good, but if I wanted to get there, I would specifically avoid your bays and harbors. The whole coast, so I have read, is sandy beach, free from strong sea wind and offering good anchorage. There I would make my landing and catch you unaware from behind; how would that suit you?

NEW NETHERLANDER: It is easy to say that but impossible to do. True, by taking some risk you might get to some or other place, beach your vessel, and go ashore, but you would not have achieved anything since the entire coast of New Netherland is of double formation. In between are wide and shallow waters, or there are offshore islands, in some places two or three deep. If you are willing to ignore and overlook those sounds and islands, then tell me where you would obtain a boat for passing over and through them. It is a job for a madman; all in all it cannot be done in that way. And suppose someone were to attempt such a stunt, we should know of it before he landed, from the Indians who roam along the beaches and are wont to claim a messenger's fee when they spy ships off the coast.

PATRIOT: But what about Long Island?

NEW NETHERLANDER: There nothing is to be done either, for Long Island, for the most part, has a double coastline as well. Assume you are on it, how do you get off again, or what advantage can you gain, surely nothing but greater damage and danger. If anything were to be achieved, it would have to be at New Amsterdam. And if you reply, that is where you want to be, I ask you to consider, first, that you can hardly get there owing to the unfamiliar sailing channel, and next, that we should always know of it a day or two ahead. At any semblance of danger we should immediately fortify Sandy Hook and The Narrows. Then there is Fort Amsterdam itself, under whose cannon you cannot avoid passing. It carries so much artillery that, in my judgment, half of it will not need to be engaged to repel whatever forces may thus approach in the next fifty years.

PATRIOT: All right, that seems adequate for dealing with outside forces arriving by sea, but inland you have the Indians, and on both sides the English in great numbers. You well know the danger of having such testy and powerful neighbors; what have you to say to that?

NEW NETHERLANDER: As regards the aborigines, or Indians, that does not amount to much; they can now see for themselves that their doings mean very little, no more than it takes to dumbfound some rascal or a newcomer who knows no better. Read the chapter "Of Their Warfare," in the *Description of New Netherland,* and you will see that they cannot form up in regiments, companies, or platoons, and have too little authority over one another for their efforts to have any effect. And second, the war recently fought against them, when we had not half the strength in men we have now, is so well remembered by them that they will not lightly start anything; if we were to speak of how it began, though, on that occasion the Indians could hardly be blamed, but that is over and done with.

As far as the English are concerned, the situation is disquieting and has already caused difficulties. I can tell you that we in New Netherland may yet, if it be not presumptuous, so concern ourselves with the war that in consequence we may provoke a confrontation with the Virginians and the New Englanders.[1]

PATRIOT: Provoke?—Man, we should have much preferred to stay out of it, but it seems one cannot have peace and quiet for longer than his neighbors are willing to have it.

NEW NETHERLANDER: That is not so evident, nor do I know how matters stand between you and them, but this I have read and can understand, too: That it is not always wise to decline taking a stand on affairs that either are necessarily for the ultimate account of one of the parties or so involve one's interests that, owing to various considerations and circumstances, he becomes the third party to the case. I could give you many examples from history, but because they all point to the same conclusion and the matter at issue is delicate, I shall for good reasons pass it by and revert to New Netherland.

In order to satisfy you in this respect as well, I maintain that the Virginians can do nothing, unless they came by sea, and on that score we have already given our answer; overland the long and rough roads and several big rivers block their way. We could do them more harm than they us. The New Englanders, it is true, are much stronger than we are, but I cannot see that therefore it would suit them better than it would us to lapse into mutual unpleasantness, since their welfare depends wholly or mainly on trade that they can hardly carry on southward from Cape Cod without passing through the channel behind Long Island. Next, they live in open country and are dispersed along a hundred miles of coast without any forts, soldiers, or armed forces, and armaments, other than having exercised their planters and residents to be able to resist the Indians. If we suffered any provocation from them, they must be aware that with few men—fewer than we in New Netherland can release for the purpose—we can send parties to disturb the peace throughout their country, seeing that they have numerous small villages that can offer little or no resistance. These are situated in or next to forests, where one can start fires, plunder everything, and promptly disappear again into the woods without a trace. Therefore, I have little fear of them.

Nor will they do anything of that nature without an express command from parliament, which will not lightly resolve on it, for by doing so the reprisals might well escalate to a declared open war with England, which is no more desired there than it is here. And as long as you cannot make me believe that the New Englanders are insane, you cannot convince me either that they will make war on us or affront us in such manner. I attribute this not so much to their goodwill as to their own gain and profit that depend on the present situation and the great risk of going under if they acted otherwise.

As to your Portuguese or pirates, that is a minor hazard, as can be inferred from what has been said. Assuming some pirate sneaked in, what of it? The man could frankly count on heading for his grave, because he would have far fewer ships and foot soldiers, and we should nab him before he could do any mischief.

As regards what you choose to say of our nation, I realize they are inclined to truck and trade. Speaking of everyone individually you may be right, but sir, let us make a distinction here between individual persons at large and an established government: Where in the world is there a government more disposed to improve on nature with man's handiwork and to fortify and secure its territory than ours, and where under the sun are there people who contribute more liberally to it than our nation? Still, it must be financed, and everyone must be free to have his say in the matter even though it would often be better to remain silent. Thus, to discuss New Netherland in that context with the government people over there, recommendations need to be formulated and sent over, and detailed instructions must be given by the superior authorities here. Then the approval of the community must be sought as soon as can be and in light of their mood, in order to readily obtain the necessary requisitions from them, as is the practice in this country in similar cases. That, so to say, is how it goes generally, save in special circumstances. When present need counsels dispatch, however, the law must be shaped by the situation. With that, dear sir, I think your firm conclusions will have been appreciably weakened.

PATRIOT: I must with some reluctance admit that I had not fully understood all of it, and that the problem is not as great as I thought. Let us leave that to one side now and speak of trade. Tell me, please, what it mostly consists in and what, with a growing population, it could eventually comprise.

NEW NETHERLANDER: I am pleased that I have to a degree satisfied you thus far, and on this, the third topic, I reckon I can convince you best.

PATRIOT: Places that are useful to us must support trade and offer scope for it; otherwise they do not interest us, be the soil and lands ever so good. In Germany, the Duchy of Brandenburg and the Palatinate, and other parts nearer by, have land and good soil galore, but that is to no avail, for with their limited trading opportunities they cannot prosper.

NEW NETHERLANDER: Trade is the object, and on trade we must depend. The trade carried on in New Netherland right now is mostly in grains such as wheat, rye, peas, barley, etc. Also bacon, meat, fish, beer, wine, and whatever else is supplied to the household and the table or for consumption. All that is plentiful, so that quantities of it can be shipped out by way of the good navigable streams we have, of which more later, to the islands as well as the West Indies. We have long been providing significant support to those places with foodstuffs from New Netherland. The more the population increases, the more ample supply we shall have of everything, since newcomers provide for themselves in the second year, and in the third they already produce some surplus. Further we have tobacco and the goods we get in return for the said foodstuffs, and these can be fairly important. Also a variety of peltries such as beaver, otter, bear, elk, and deer skins, as can be seen in the *Description*. Wine farming is only beginning to progress and, in time, will be of some account. So will deep-sea fishing; should you require a hundred shiploads of fish, you may depend on obtaining it if you make the effort. Throughout winter, train oil can be boiled in the South Bay from the whales who come there in large numbers. Next, there is available, or can be had in quantity timber, hemp, tar, ashes, iron, etc., about which the *Description* can inform you fully. And now, in order to dispose of the trade issue, I am going to present three arguments to you, and then we shall see at once how matters stand.

[First,] it is now only about fifteen years since New Netherland began to be properly settled and visited by private individuals. In that time we had to endure that pernicious war; without it we should have been as far advanced ever since then as we are now, for what had been built up prior to that campaign by the company was either of small account, apart from the forts and some dwellings, or was destroyed in the war.[2] No persons of means have come over, save a few quite recently. Everyone who came wanted to gain much and bring in nothing, while the merchants, who did bring some goods with them, took away incomparably more. The way it goes in new places, at first you have few churchwardens, but instead people who are good at lining their pockets and not particularly attentive to the end result or to the promotion of the commonweal—no offense meant to the good ones. Still, if you were there now, you would see before you, and seeing is believing, many fine, decent people living well in good order and style. Likewise, many handsome houses, well built and furnished; good farms, plantations, pastures, cornfields, gardens, and orchards; and with goodly herds of a variety of cattle. If the land were anything but good, where would all that have come from, for nothing worthwhile can be got from what is not good in itself.

Second, if one were to say to that, sure, but it is costing individuals, the company, and others plenty of money, we should reply that never has anything been consigned to New Netherland that was not recouped together with a pretty fair profit. You may think that surprising, because so many accounts are still in arrears, but I do not say that all was returned to its rightful owners, for then I should be speaking against my better knowledge. Just consider how many peltries were alienated from the company in the time before trade was opened up, as you can best ascertain by comparing what passed through in those years with what is now coming through, although not all of it is publicly declared even now; in later years little or no shortfall occurred. Informed persons know that not a quarter of the profit made on company merchandise flowed into the company's coffers, yet when a loss was incurred, it was borne by the company alone. Many and high salaries had to be provided for, but cashiers and loafers who acted the libertine and made good cheer embezzled the money left and right. It did them little good, for money tends to go the way it came. The point I wish to make is that a fair amount was earned in New Netherland that is not outwardly apparent, because it was squandered again or still supports a good living in this country. Nevertheless, it originated there or was earned from local sources.

And third, the country is truly suited and well situated for commerce: One, because it has fine and fertile land on which everything grows aplenty; two, because its fine rivers and navigable waterways reach many places and enable produce to be collected for purposes of trading; three, because the Indians, without labor and exertion on our part, provide us with a handsome and considerable peltry trade that can be assessed at several tons of gold annually. It is as though that were earned for us over and above the meat and corn for which we also have to thank them; and four, because the country's situation on the coast is as good as that of any other, which for that reason alone is regarded as rich and fortunate. To the northeast are the valuable Newfoundland fishing grounds, easily reached in four or five days' sailing. Canada and New England are within brief sailing time along coastal waterways. New Netherland already trades with those territories, and in time, and with a growing population, trade can expand still more. To the southwest lies Virginia, with a substantial tobacco trade. Then there is Florida, with the Bahama Channel and all the islands and mainland of the West Indies, whose trade is of some importance.

PATRIOT: But in terms of the peace treaty we cannot mention those latter parts, for the ports of either party are closed to the other, so that given the circumstances nothing can be undertaken there.[3]

NEW NETHERLANDER: I admit it, and also believe that if all our principals had been fully aware of the benefit for the state of not closing the ports, and how notably that would have restored the fortunes of the West India Company, it would not have come to closure or they would have stipulated nonclosure.

PATRIOT: Oh, sir, you err. The matter was not neglected and enough diplomatic efforts were made, but without success, and it could not be avoided.

NEW NETHERLANDER: Diplomatic effort, yes, I do not dispute that. But the king of Spain's position was that he could not or dared not omit it, unless we undertook to keep away from his mines. We might still have arranged somehow as a second best to trade through Spanish commission agents and so gradually make some progress; now I see not much chance of it. That is how it stands, but we in New Netherland are confident that, provided we become stronger and more populous, we can manage to capture that trade, albeit on a commission basis on whatever terms. We believe we know what means to use, and they cannot really refuse or prevent us, for the island of Curaçao, which falls under New Netherland, is not far distant from Cartagena, and by reliable report, a mere eight miles from, and within sight of, the mainland coast.

Apart from all that, we have so much merchandise, more than we can use up, available for trading with the Caribbean islands, which are always a good market. That trade will grow and expand accordingly as our power and wealth increase. Therefore we need have no fear, as certain pessimistic persons have put it to me, that even though New Netherland yielded much good produce, we should be unable to sell or do business with it.

And finally, what would prevent the New Netherlanders from trading with France, Spain, Portugal, and the entire Mediterranean equally well as from this country, given the men and the means? A growing population will infallibly supply those two requisites even if, in a manner of speaking, no other people went there than those who had merely their bare limbs to see them through; the country would soon enough yield them clothing and a living.

PATRIOT: I can tell you what will prevent their doing so, and that is distance. Not only do you lack the means for doing business over there; you could not procure consignments and provisions in those parts either, such as you can here.

NEW NETHERLANDER: True, sir, and we are now looking

too far ahead, but the distance cannot save your argument, because we can sail from there with one and the same wind and on the same course, across a free and wide-open sea, without concern for or danger of sand, rock, or enemy, to all of the Atlantic coast of Europe as it extends from Ireland down to the Strait [of Gibraltar] in four weeks or less, barring adverse conditions. Therefore, it makes little difference, because what you gain on the one hand you lose on the other.

In conclusion, a territory like New Netherland, so suitable for commerce, as we have seen, which from its own resources produces assorted goods and requisites and has a surplus for supplying to others, must it not, given appropriate initiatives and direction, eventually prosper?—Judge for yourself.

PATRIOT: I can well see that, and it would not be a bad plan, with the right measures, to develop that country, but more of this on a future occasion. My questions thus far I consider now to have been answered, and if anything further were to occur to me later, do me the honor of allowing me to ask.

NEW NETHERLANDER: That will have to be in New Netherland then, for my journey is close at hand, which leaves me little more free time to enjoy your company.

PATRIOT: Well then, depart thither again this season; it shows that you do not find it unpleasant there.

NEW NETHERLANDER: God willing, such is my firm design. With that I take for the time being my leave.

PATRIOT: Well, sir, I pray that the Lord our God grant you a safe and speedy journey, and bestow his gracious blessing in this world and the next on you and yours and all who dwell in New Netherland, to the greatness and praise of his glorious name. Amen.

APPENDIX

*A List and Suggested Identification
of the Latinized Plant Names
Recorded by Adriaen van der Donck*

Unless otherwise noted, listed species are native. The plants appear in the order mentioned in the book.

Capilli veneris = *Adiantum capillus-veneris,* common maidenhair fern, not found in the Northeast. The native species in the area is northern maidenhair fern, *A. pedatum.*

Scholopentria = *Scolopendria,* a species name for a tropical fern. Within the lower forty-eight states one species is present, the introduced monarch fern, *Phymatosorus scolopendria,* found only in Florida.

Angelica = *Angelica atropurpurea,* purple-stem angelica; *A. lucida,* seacoast angelica; or *A. venenosa,* hairy angelica.

Polupodium = *Polypodium,* a widespread genus of ferns represented in the Northeast by *Polypodium virginianum,* rock polypody, and *P. appalachianum,* Appalachian polypody.

Verbascum album = *Verbascum blattaria, V. phlomoides, V. thapsus, V. lychnitis,* and others, common name mullein, all introduced Old World species.

Calteus sacerdotis = Unknown, but perhaps intending the genus *Caltha,* as in *Caltha palustris,* the yellow marsh marigold.

Atriplex hortense and *marine* = *Atriplex hortensis,* garden orache, an introduced plant. *Marine* is unknown. *Atriplex* is the genus name for the native saltbush.

Chortium = Unknown.

Turrites = *Turritis glabra,* also *Arabis glabra,* tower rockcress.

Calamus aromaticus = *Acorus calamus*, an introduced plant also known
as *A. aromaticus* and *A. americanus*, common name sweetflag.

Sassafrax = *Sassafras albidum*, the sassafras tree, the root bark of
which produces oil of sassafras, widely believed to be a cure-all.

Rois virginianum = Unknown.

Ranunculus = *Ranunculus abortivus*, *R. hispidus*, *R. pensylvanicus*, *R.
trychophyllus*, and others; buttercup.

Plantago = Native and introduced plants of the genus *Plantago*, plantain or common plantain.

Burso pastoris = *Capsella bursa-pastoris*, shepherd's purse, an introduced plant.

Malva = Several introduced species of variously named mallows of
the genus *Malva*.

Origaenum = May intend *Origanum vulgare*, oregano, or *O. majorana*,
sweet marjoram, both introduced species.

Gheranicum = Perhaps one of several native species of the genus
Geranium, namely Bicknell's cranesbill, in addition to Carolina,
Robert, and also spotted geraniums.

Althea = Marshmallow, an introduced species of the genus *Althaea*.

Cinoroton psuydo = Unknown.

Daphine = May intend the genus *Daphne*, in this case *Daphne
mezereum*, the introduced paradise plant.

Viola = The genus *Viola*, violets, of which there are many species
present in the Northeast.

Ireas = Iris, of the genus *Iris*, with several native and introduced
species in the Northeast.

Indigo silvestris = Perhaps *Amorpha fruticosa*, indigo bush, also called
false indigo, or *Baptisia australis*, blue wild indigo, also not a
true indigo.

Sigilum salamonis = Solomon's seal, *Polygonatum biflorum*, var. *com-
mutatum*, and *P. pubescens*.

Sanguis dracoum = Sanguis draconis, or "dragon's blood," scientific
name *Daemomorops draco*. A plant native to Indonesia, where in
the early seventeenth century the United East India Company
(voc) had established a lively and profitable trade, that produces a
red resinous substance used as a dye; it also was regarded to have

medicinal qualities. It may be that the Dutch had imported the plant and were attempting to grow it in New Netherland.

Consolidae = Probably comfrey, genus *Symphytum*, also known as *Consolidae radix*, an introduced species.

Mille folium = *Achillea millefolium*, yarrow, with one introduced and three native varieties in the region.

Noli metanghere = The touch-me-not, genus *Impatiens*, which includes jewelweed and the pale touch-me-not.

Cardo benedictus = *Carduus benedictus*, better known as *Cnicus benedictus*, the introduced blessed thistle.

Agrunonium = Agrimony, represented by several species of the genus *Agrimonia*, one of which is introduced.

Serpentanae = *Gutierrezia sarothrae*, broom snakeweed.

Elaetine = Waterwort, three species of the genus *Elatine*.

Camperfoelie = The plant family Caprifoliaceae, genus *Lonicera*, honeysuckle, represented in the Northeast by several native and introduced species.

Petum (also *petun* and *pitum*) = A name of native Brazilian origin for tobacco, borrowed by Europeans in the seventeenth century (OED). In 1632 Samuel de Champlain called the Khionontateronon—an Iroquoian-speaking group located on the south end of Norrawasaga Bay, Ontario—the Petun after observing that these Indians grew and traded tobacco. See Charles Garrad and Conrad E. Heidenreich, "Khionontateronon (Petun)," in *Handbook of North American Indians*, vol. 15, *Northeast*, ed. Bruce G. Trigger (Washington DC: Smithsonian Institution, 1978), 396.

NOTES

All notes are the editors'.

Preface

1. Adriaen van Der Donck, *A Description of the New Netherlands*, ed. Thomas F. O'Donnell (Syracuse NY: Syracuse University Press, 1968), xl.
2. Ada van Gastel, "Van der Donck's Description of the Indians: Additions and Corrections," *William and Mary Quarterly* 47, no. 3 (1990): 411–21. For Van Gastel's analysis of Van der Donck's career in the New World, see "Adriaen van der Donck, New Netherland, and America" (PhD diss., Pennsylvania State University, 1985).

The Country

1. Van der Donck's "mile" (Dutch, *mijl*) approximates 2.8 statute miles.
2. In 1602 the States General of the United Provinces of the Netherlands chartered the VOC (Verenigde Oost-indische Compagnie), or United East India Company, to manage the lucrative trade with the Far East. Formed as a joint stock company, it was given the authority to raise its own army and navy in order to maintain control of its trade routes. Moreover, in these endeavors it held the power to make war and peace and also to negotiate treaties with foreign princes. Essentially, the VOC represented the privatization of Dutch foreign policy. See note 7.
3. In 1638 Sweden chartered the South Company to form a colony in the New World. The first director was Peter Minuit, former

director of New Netherland. He purchased land in the area of Wilmington, Delaware, and constructed a fort named Christina after Sweden's reigning monarch. The colony expanded southward in 1654 when a Swedish relief expedition captured Fort Casimir, at present New Castle, Delaware, from the Dutch. Although the Swedes had gained control of the entire river, the colony remained weak because of irregular resupply from the home country. In 1655 Petrus Stuyvesant brought the Swedish colony under Dutch control.

4. Selected Native oral traditions concerned with the arrival of Europeans are discussed in James Axtell, "Through Another Glass Darkly: Early Indian Views of Europeans," in *After Columbus: Essays in the Ethnohistory of Colonial North America* (New York: Oxford University Press, 1988), 125–43. Van der Donck, however, was using the story he alleges the Indians told him to buttress Dutch claims of discovery to New Netherland. These were asserted in the face of competing claims by England and, until 1655, when its colony of New Sweden in the lower Delaware Valley was taken by the Dutch, also Sweden.

5. Corn and beans are New World domesticates, with corn (*Zea mays amylacea* and *Zea mays indurata*) appearing in the Northeast ten centuries or more before the arrival of the Dutch, and beans (*Phaseolus vulgaris*) about AD 1000. "Turkish corn," also Turkish wheat, Welsh corn, Indian wheat, and others, was a term for corn in common use among seventeenth-century Europeans.

6. The *Remonstrance* is a lengthy and detailed representation, a protest by aggrieved citizens about conditions in the colony, written by Van der Donck and submitted to the States General in 1649. For the complete text, see E. B. O'Callaghan, ed., *Documents Relative to the Colonial History of the State of New-York; Procured in Holland, England and France, by John Romeyn Brodhead*, 15 vols. (Albany NY: Weed, Parsons, 1853–87), 1:271–318. For all intents and purposes, the *Representation* is a first draft of Van der Donck's *A Description of New Netherland*, in particular the sections on physical geography, natural history, and also Indian

life ways. See note 7. Modeled on the East India Company, the West India Company was chartered in 1621 to carry on the war with Spain after the expiration of the Twelve Years' Truce (1609–21). Its area of control was vast, extending from the west coast of Africa westward to the easternmost reaches of the Indonesian archipelago. The WIC's primary interests were with Africa for its gold, ivory, and slaves; Brazil for its sugar and dyewood; the Caribbean for its salt; and New Netherland for its furs.

7. The States General was the governing body of the United Provinces of the Netherlands. Each of the seven provinces sent representatives to The Hague, where matters of state were decided. The States General is immortalized in many placenames around the world, including New York's Staten Island.

8. Early on, Long Island Sound was called the East River.

9. The reference is to the Swedes of the Delaware Valley who chose to remain and work for the West India Company after the Dutch takeover of New Sweden in 1655. See the report of Augustine Herrman's embassy to Maryland in 1659 in Charles T. Gehring, trans. and ed., *Delaware Papers (Dutch Period): A Collection of Documents Pertaining to the Regulation of Affairs on the South River of New Netherland, 1648–1664* (Baltimore MD: Genealogical Publishing, 1981), 222.

10. At Trenton, New Jersey.

11. The two whales, one white and one brown, appeared in the Hudson River before Fort Orange. Both swam as far north as present Troy, creating a stir among the population. So unusual was their appearance that Anthony de Hooghes, secretary of Rensselaerswijck, made special note of the event in his memorandum book.

12. Rensselaerswijck was a one-million-acre agricultural colony on the upper Hudson, comprising roughly present Albany and Rensselaer counties. Known as a patroonship, it was the WIC's attempt to privatize colonization. Well-connected and wealthy individuals—patroons—were allowed to acquire from presumed rightful owners land on which they were to establish a certain

number of settlers within a prescribed period of time. In return the patroon was given administrative, executive, and judicial rights over his colony and allowed to pass the patroonship on to his heirs.

13. The "river of Canada," or St. Lawrence River, is mentioned several times in Van der Donck's narrative. In the strict context of the geography here, however, the river is the Richelieu, which flows from Lake Champlain into the St. Lawrence.

14. Described is present Lake Champlain, 110 miles in length, 12 miles wide, and containing some eighty islands. A portage of about 10 miles would have been required between present Fort Edward and Lake George; a much shorter one to Lake Champlain, thence to the Richelieu River and the St. Lawrence.

15. The actual height of Cohoes Falls is about sixty-five feet.

16. The Maquas and the Scimekas are the Mohawks and the "Sinnekens," the latter term one the Dutch initially applied to the Oneidas. Charles T. Gehring and William A. Starna, trans. and eds., *A Journey into Mohawk and Oneida Country, 1634–1635: The Journal of Harmen Meyndertsz van den Bogaert* (Syracuse NY: Syracuse University Press, 1988), 14. On occasion, *Sinnekens* was used as a collective for Indians living west of the Mohawks, namely the Oneidas, the Onondagas, the Cayugas, and the Senecas. Only later was it applied and restricted to the westernmost group, the Senecas. See Ives Goddard's synomomy in Thomas S. Abler and Elisabeth Tooker, "Seneca," in *Handbook of North American Indians*, vol. 15, *Northeast*, ed. Bruce G. Trigger (Washington DC: Smithsonian Institution, 1978), 515. The lake referred to here is Oneida Lake, which nevertheless is not the source of the Mohawk River.

17. Indians inhabiting the Mohawk Valley traveled the river in dugouts or in canoes fashioned of tree bark, presumably from the American elm. J. Franklin Jameson, ed., *Narratives of New Netherland, 1609–1664* (New York: Charles Scribner's Sons, 1909), 176. This imposing tree has since been devastated by a pathogen, a fungus, introduced into North America in about 1930. Interestingly enough, it was first identified by a Dutch biologist, hence its name, Dutch elm disease.

18. Probably a reference to the sulfur, magnesia, and chalybeate mineral springs at present Sharon Springs, fifty miles west of Albany, in Mohawk country.

19. "Highlands" carries with it two meanings, one geographic and the other cultural. As Van der Donck notes, it is the mountainous and hilly regions bordering both sides of the river from about Poughkeepsie south to the lower valley, although the Dutch at times favored the west side with this name. See Jameson, *Narratives*, 206. There also were "Highland Indians," Wappingers and other Munsee speakers whose lands stretched along the east side of the valley from about southern Dutchess County into Westchester County. Ives Goddard, "Delaware," in Trigger, *Handbook*, 15:237.

20. Many long, narrow, and flat islands could be found throughout much of the river's length.

21. A *morgen* is a Dutch land measurement of about two acres.

22. *Wilden*: "wild one," here "Indian." Regarding the Indian's reference to "grain," the likelihood is that the Indians had planted corn, a grain, at this spot.

23. The east side of the patroonship was called Grenebosch, which translates as "pinewoods"; under the English it developed into Greenbush, surviving in the placenames East and North Greenbush and Green Island.

24. The American chestnut (*Castanea dentata*), which produced an edible fruit. It is gone from eastern forests, the victim of a blight that began in New York City in 1904.

25. The name "water beech," also known as the American hornbeam, is misapplied. Described is the American sycamore, also called the American plane tree (*Platanus occidentalis*). The tree equivalent to the European linden is the American basswood (*Tilia americana*).

26. Indians in the Hudson Valley and southern New England, including Long Island, greater New York, and New Jersey, commonly used the tulip tree, also called the yellow poplar, in addition to the white pine, the chestnut, and the eastern cottonwood, to manufacture dugout canoes, often of considerable

size, the preferred watercraft of these areas. See Jameson, *Narratives*, 48, 57.

27. "Crab" is probably the sweet crab apple (*Pyrus coronaria*).

28. The nut trees to which Van der Donck refers may be the black walnut (*Juglans nigra*) or perhaps the butternut (*Juglans cinerea*), comparing these species to the English walnut (*Juglans regia*). Prickly pears: eastern prickly pear cactus (*Opuntia compressa*), also known as Indian fig.

29. "Artichokes" likely refers to the Jerusalem artichoke (*Helianthus tuberosus*), a member of the sunflower family. "Earth chestnuts" are possibly the hog peanut (*Amphicarpa bracteata*), which produces edible seeds in underground pods, a food source known to Indian people throughout the east.

30. The native fox grape and several other species of wild grapes.

31. For "dragon's blood," see the appendix.

32. Both are loan words. *Quaesiens* is basically English "squash," shortened within English from a southeastern New England Algonquian word (Narragansett, *askútasquash*). *Cascoeten* is also "squash" but from Unquachog, *áscoot*, with the Dutch plural ending *-ens*. Ives Goddard, Smithsonian Institution, personal communication, August 3, 2005. The modern Mohawk equivalent is *onon'ónsera'*, "squash." Van der Donck is referring to summer squash, *Cucurbita pepo*, although Indians in the region also grew another variety of *C. pepo*, the common pumpkin.

33. Citrullines: *Citrullus*, the genus within which are several species of watermelon, citron.

34. Calabash: also known as the bottle gourd (*Lagenaria siceraria*). *Skipple*: a dry measure equivalent to two-thirds of a bushel.

35. The word *tessen* is unidentified.

36. The most common variety was the kidney bean (*Phaseolus vulgaris*), followed by the scarlet runner (*Phaseolus multiflorus*) and perhaps others. See F. W. Waugh, *Iroquois Foods and Food Preparation*, Memoirs of the Canadian Geological Survey 86, Anthropological Series 12 (1916; repr., Ottawa, 1973), 103–4.

37. Van der Donck's comment that violets were an introduced flower is incorrect; there are many native species present in the Northeast.

38. "Spanish fig" is probably a European term for the eastern prickly pear cactus. See note 28. For an analysis of this list of plants, see the appendix.

39. See the appendix.

40. *Beer* can designate either a bear or a boar in Dutch. Misguided by the pronunciation, the English mistakenly renamed it Barren Island. It is located in the Hudson River at the southern limit of Rensselaerswijck.

41. Augustijn Heermans was a multitalented Bohemian who served the WIC in various capacities. The view of New Amsterdam on the map of New Netherland is attributed to Heermans (also Herrman). In 1659 Stuyvesant sent him on a mission to Maryland to resolve a boundary dispute in the South River (the Delaware) region of New Netherland. Heermans's knowledge of the area and skills as a diplomat so impressed his English counterparts that he was hired to make a map of the Chesapeake. What he produced was held in such high regard that he was given a large land grant on the upper Chesapeake Bay known as Bohemia Manor. New Amsterdam is present New York City.

42. Born in Wesel (present Germany) of Huguenot parents, Minuit originally served in New Netherland as a volunteer under Willem Verhulst, the first full-time director. In 1626 Minuit was appointed director, in which position he served until 1632. His recall was initiated by a faction that opposed the patroonship plan of colonization. Minuit's knowledge of the region attracted the attention of investors in Sweden interested in establishing a colony in the New World. So it was that in 1638 he led an expedition to the Delaware River, where he purchased land for the Swedish South Company. While on his return voyage to Sweden, by way of the island of St. Christopher, present St. Kitts in the British West Indies, Minuit was invited to dine aboard a Dutch vessel moored in the harbor. A severe storm, perhaps a hurricane, struck the area, forcing ships to sea. There Minuit and *Het vliegende Hert* (The Flying Stag), the ship he was on, were lost.

43. In 1631 the WIC began its conquest of Portuguese Brazil north

of the Rio Francisco. This expensive operation was made possible by Piet Hein's capture of the Spanish silver fleet in 1628. WIC interest in Brazil was sugar, which had become a much-sought-after commodity in Europe. Portugal regained control of its lost territory when the Dutch surrendered Recife, the capital of New Holland, in 1654.

44. "Peas" refers to the Old World field pea, also called the garden pea (*Pisum sativum*).

45. From 1 Samuel 17:17. The roasted grain mentioned in this biblical passage was not corn.

46. An Amsterdam measure, or *skipple*, equals roughly three-quarters of a bushel.

47. The Reverend Johannes Megapolensis was hired by Kiliaen van Rensselaer in 1642 to serve as minister to Rensselaerswijck for six years. Megapolensis is a Greco-Latinization of Van Grootstede, his family name. His familiarity with the local Indians inspired him to write "A Short Account of the Mohawk Indians" in 1644. Jameson, *Narratives*, 168–80. Upon expiration of his contract in 1648, he attempted to return to the Netherlands but was persuaded by Petrus Stuyvesant to fill the recently vacated pulpit on Manhattan, which he did until his death in 1669.

48. See Jameson, *Narratives*, 170.

49. Brandt Pelen was one of the first farmers recruited by Kiliaen van Rensselaer in 1630; he managed a farm on Castle Island (the present Port of Albany) in Rensselaerswijck until his death in 1644. *Schepen*: an appointed official of a municipality with administrative and judicial authority. New Amsterdam's municipal government consisted of two burgomasters and five *schepens*.

50. An employee of Michael Pauw's patroonship of Pavonia, Jan Evertsz Bout was granted a lease to establish a farm near Ahasimus (present Jersey City) in 1638.

51. An ell is twenty-seven inches.

52. Varinas is a Venezuelan tobacco.

53. Willem Kieft served as director of New Netherland from 1638 to 1647. He is most infamously known for his war with the Indians of the lower Hudson, 1643–45. Kieft drowned while re-

turning to the Netherlands in 1647 aboard the WIC ship *Princess Amalia*, which wrecked off the coast of Wales near Swansea.

54. "The Raritans" refers to the region surrounding New Jersey's Raritan River, home of the Raritan Indians. Jameson, *Narratives*, 208. In *Novum Belgium*, describing events in 1643 and 1644, the Jesuit Father Isaac Jogues writes of a reported gold mine "toward" the Delaware River. In 1645 mineral specimens thought valuable, taken from a mountain "near the *Raretang*," were delivered to the Dutch. The Kittatinny Mountains area of Warren County, New Jersey, has yielded traces of gold in auriferous pyrite, and also silver, although not in economically recoverable amounts. Reuben Gold Thwaites, ed., *The Jesuit Relations and Allied Documents: Travels and Explorations of the Jesuit Missionaries in New France, 1610–1691*, 73 vols. (Cleveland: Burrows Brothers, 1896–1901), 28:108; O'Callaghan, *Documents Relative*, 13:19; James Greenfield Manchester, *The Minerals of New York City and Its Environs*, Bulletin of the New York Mineralogical Club, vol. 3, no. 1 (New York: Afferton, 1931), 79.

55. In early summer 1645, Kieft traveled to Fort Orange to meet with Mohawks, Mahicans, and other unnamed natives. A record of this conference, along with a nineteenth-century translation, was lost in the 1911 New York State Library fire; however, a summary based on these materials appears in E. B. O'Callaghan, *History of New Netherland; or, New York under the Dutch*, 2 vols. (New York: D. Appleton, 1846), 1:355–56.

56. "Agheroense" is a Mohawk name; thus he was a Mohawk Indian.

57. Johannes La Montagne was a council member under Kieft beginning in 1638; he was appointed vice director of Fort Orange/Beverwijck in 1656.

58. Arent Corsen was a merchant from Amsterdam residing in Virginia. In 1641 he was supercargo on the ship *Eijckenboom* (Oak Tree). After departing New Haven with a collection of maps of New Netherland in 1646, both he and the ship were presumed lost at sea. Corsen's widow later petitioned to marry Johannes La Montagne.

59. The WIC ship *Princess Amalia* arrived in New Amsterdam in 1647 with Petrus Stuyvesant on board. On its return voyage the ship ran aground off the coast of Wales near Swansea and broke up on the rocks. Among the eighty-two passengers lost were former director Willem Kieft, Domine Everardus Bogardus, many WIC soldiers returning from Brazil via New Netherland, in addition to administrative papers to defend Kieft's Indian policy and ore samples. See note 53.

60. Cornelis van Tienhoven was one of the longest-tenured employees of the WIC in New Netherland, serving as bookkeeper, 1633–47; surveyor, 1647–55; receiver general, 1649–52; provincial secretary, 1651; *schout fiscal* (attorney general), 1652–56; in addition to several appointments as a special emissary and commissioner. Faced with the possibility of indictment for embezzlement, Van Tienhoven threw his hat and cane into the East River and disappeared. No one was fooled by this deception, although his name does not appear in the records again.

That the substance with which Agheroense painted his face yielded anything resembling nuggets of gold is not believable. Moreover, Van der Donck's assertion that the tests Van Tienhoven had ordered performed were positive is contradicted by a letter from the directors in Amsterdam to the council of New Netherland written just prior to April 1647: "The specimens of *New-Netherland* minerals, sent over, have been examined, but, we are told, no metal has been found in them." O'Callaghan, *Documents Relative*, 13:21, also 14:76–77; Charles T. Gehring, trans. and ed., *Correspondence 1647–1653* (Syracuse NY: Syracuse University Press, 2000), 4. There is, nonetheless, confirmed gold north of the Hoosic River in the Taconic Mountains of Washington County, New York, although amounts are minute. The source material is alluvial and may have been transported glacially. William M. Kelly, New York State Museum, personal communication, July 19, 2005, August 4, 2005.

61. Mountain crystal: quartz crystals or perhaps garnet. Glass such as comes from Moscovy: sheet mica. Gray hearthstone: possibly steatite, also known as soapstone.

62. Carbon black scraped from the bottom of cooking pots is reported to have been one source of black pigment, although a glittering paint could also be produced from charcoal. There is no direct evidence to identify the minerals that Indians in the region may have used to make pigments. The most likely candidates are red, ranging to brown; ochres (hematite, goethite), which can be iridescent; yellow ochre (limonite); and manganese, which produces dark colors, all found at locales in the Hudson and the Mohawk valleys and on Long Island. These and other pigments or dyes extracted from plants were usually mixed with animal fats or oil made from sunflower seeds, and then applied. Father Joseph François Lafitau, *Customs of the American Indians Compared with the Customs of Primitive Times*, trans. and ed. William N. Fenton and Elizabeth L. Moore, 2 vols. (Toronto: Champlain Society, 1977), 2:42; Elisabeth Tooker, *An Ethnography of the Huron Indians, 1615–1649*, Bureau of American Ethnology Bulletin 190 (Washington DC: Bureau of American Ethnology, 1964), 21.

63. Pokeweed (*Phytolacca americana*), which produces a dark purple berry. Norton G. Miller, New York State Museum, personal communication, July 18, 2005. It was widely used by Indians in the Northeast to make a paint.

64. This account of preparing dye is unique in the literature on Indians of northeastern North America.

65. "Castle" is a term the Dutch applied to palisaded/fortified Mohawk villages. Gehring and Starna, *Journey*, 3.

66. Ball-headed war clubs were a ubiquitous weapon of Native people in the Northeast. Shields made of willow, tree bark, and covered with skins are reported for Iroquoians and also Native groups in New England. See Jameson, *Narratives*, 225; Gabriel Sagard[-Théodat], *The Long Journey to the Country of the Hurons*, ed. George M. Wrong, trans. H. H. Langton (1632; repr., New York: Greenwood, 1968), 154; Lafitau, *Customs*, 2:115; Daniel Gookin, *An Historical Account of the Doings and Sufferings of the Christian Indians in New England in the Years 1675, 1676, 1677* (1836; repr., New York: Arno, 1972), 12.

67. Described are hairpieces (headdresses) in the form of fillets or garlands made of dyed deer hair, worn by Indian men. See "Of the Original Natives of New Netherland," note 12.

68. Writing in 1626, Nicolaes van Wassenaer reported that twenty cattle put out to pasture on Manhattan had died, possibly from having "eaten something bad from an uncultivated soil." Jameson, *Narratives*, 83. What Van der Donck describes may be frothy bloat, where gases associated with ruminal fermentation create a foam that prevents the animal from belching. If the malady is untreated, death by suffocation can result. This condition can occur when cattle consume forages, either pasture or hay, dominated by immature legumes, in particular clovers. Feeding coarse hay is one method of prevention, which could explain the use by the Dutch of hay grown on salt wetlands. Salty soils tend to favor the growth of grasses rather than legumes. Lorin Dean Warnick, College of Veterinary Medicine, Cornell University, personal communication, August 8, 2005.

69. The mountain lion (*Felis concolor*).

70. From Genesis 27:1–41.

71. Bears do, in fact, suck or lick their paws late in hibernation, apparently to sooth and toughen tender foot pads from which old calluses have sloughed off. Such behavior, and the fact that bears sometimes ingest these discarded pieces of flesh, have led to widespread folk beliefs among American Indians and Europeans alike that this was done for nourishment, to sustain the animal through its long period of dormancy. See Lynn L. Rogers, "Shedding of Foot Pads by Black Bears during Denning," *Journal of Mammalogy* 55 (1974): 672–74; A. Irving Hallowell, "Bear Ceremonialism in the Northern Hemisphere," *American Anthropologist* 28 (1926): 27–31; James R. Masterson, "Travelers' Tales of Colonial Natural History," *Journal of American Folklore* 59 (1946): 51–52. Van der Donck may have heard such stories from Indian people or other Dutch in New Netherland or read of them in earlier accounts; for example, see William Wood, *New England's Prospect*, ed. Alden T. Vaughan (1634; repr., Amherst MA: University of Massachusetts Press, 1977), 42. An

equally likely source, however, is Pliny the Elder, mentioned by Van der Donck several times in his narrative, who observed that bears "find nourishment by sucking their fore-paws." See [Pliny the Elder,] *The Natural History of Pliny*, ed. John Bostock and Henry T. Riley, 6 vols. (London: H. G. Bohn, 1855), 2:305–7.

72. The notion that wild animals in the region might be domesticated and put to good use was not unique to Van der Donck. Writing from Massachusetts Bay two decades earlier, William Wood provided the following observations about moose: "The English have some thoughts of keeping them tame and to accustom them to the yoke, which will be a great commodity: first, because they are so fruitful, bringing forth three at a time, being likewise very uberous; secondly, because they will live in winter without fodder." Wood, *New England's Prospect*, 43.

73. Although deer populations in the region were substantial, they were not nearly as high as they are today. Also, because deer were a critical source of food and clothing, hunting them likely generated competition among neighboring Indian groups that may have resulted in conflict. Richard Michael Gramly, "Deerskins and Hunting Territories: Competition for a Scarce Resource of the Northeastern Woodlands," *American Antiquity* 42 (1977): 601–5; William A. Starna and John H. Relethford, "Deer Densities and Population Dynamics: A Cautionary Note," *American Antiquity* 50 (1985): 825–32.

74. Van der Donck did not see fallow deer (*Cervus dama*), a species only later introduced into North America from the circum-Mediterranean.

75. The Jesuit priest Isaac Jogues, first captured by Mohawks in 1642, escaped to Fort Orange the following year. With Dutch assistance he sailed to France but was back in New France by 1644. In October 1646 he revisited Mohawk country, where he was executed as a sorcerer.

76. Described is the moose.

77. The allusion to unicorns is interesting given this mythical beast's ostensible Old World origins. In 1628 Isaack De Rasieres had reported an almost identical tale from southeastern New Eng-

land: "The savages [there] say that far in the interior there are certain beasts of the size of oxen, having but one horn, which are very fierce. The English have used great diligence in order to see them, but cannot succeed therein, although they have seen the flesh and hides of them which were brought to them by the savages." Jameson, *Narratives*, 114.

78. *Loesen*: a variation of *catloes*, "lynx." Both the bobcat (*Lynx rufus*) and lynx (*Lynx lynx*) ranged throughout New Netherland. The lynx, which by the twentieth century had been nearly extirpated, is still found in parts of New England, with a few reported in extreme northern New York; bobcats remain in New York state with population centers in the Adirondack, the Catskill, and the Taconic mountains.

79. *Espannen*: Munsee, *éespan*, "raccoon." The Dutch usually wrote this word plural, *espan(n)en*, or with added *h-*, *hespan(n)en*. Ives Goddard, personal communication, January 2, 2006. *Schobben* may be a variant of *schrobben*, "to scrub," later reflected in the modern Dutch word for raccoon, *wasbeer*, literally "washing bear." The raccoon is native to North America; it was not introduced into Europe, specifically Germany, until the 1930s.

80. This is the skunk. Civet cats, or ringtails, are not found east of the Mississippi.

81. There were no badgers in the mid-Atlantic states or New England. Although Van der Donck had written *hasen*, "hares," a few lines previous, here he substitutes *trommelslagers*, "drummers," an obvious reference to the habit of hares to thump their hind feet when alarmed. This is the snowshoe hare (*Lepus americanus*).

82. Of the two species noted, the first is the golden eagle; the second, the bald eagle.

83. Swifts: Van der Donck writes *steen-krijters*, the European common swift (*Apus apus*), which is not a raptor.

84. The starling was not introduced into North America until 1890.

85. Great gray owl.

86. Twenty stivers equaled one guilder. A *daalder* equaled one and a half guilders, or thirty stivers.

87. To the best of our knowledge, this description of catching turkeys is unique in the literature.
88. The pheasant, of Old World origin, was not introduced into
the Americas until the early eighteenth century. Snipes in the
region are limited to the common snipe.
89. Sandhill crane.
90. Flocks of migratory passenger pigeons (*Ectopistes migratorius*),
which became extinct in 1914.
91. *Boompikkers*: "treepeckers."
92. Although a very shy bird, difficult to observe, the "big crest"
and large tree holes clearly point to the pileated woodpecker.
93. In 1628 De Rasieres reported, "Of the birds, there is a kind like
starlings, which we call *maize thieves*, because they do so much
damage to the maize. . . . Sometimes we take them by surprise
and fire amongst them with hailshot . . . so that sixty, seventy,
and eighty fall all at once." A similar description appears in a
small book on New Netherland by David De Vries, published
in 1655. Jameson, *Narratives*, 114, 221–22.
94. Jacob van Curler was an employee of the WIC who was ordered
by Wouter van Twiller, director of New Netherland, to establish
a presence on the Connecticut River. In 1633 he supervised the
construction of a fortified trading post called House of Hope
at the location of present Hartford.
95. Flocks of red-winged blackbirds and common grackles.
96. "White throats" is uncertain since several bird species in the
region display white throats.
97. The azure birds are probably the indigo bunting; the orange are
orioles.
98. The tundra swan, also called the whistling swan.
99. Described is the Canada goose.
100. The white-fronted goose is the least common goose to be found
today in the eastern United States.
101. Most of the fish species named by Van der Donck are found in
the Hudson River and the waters surrounding Manhattan, New
Jersey, and Long Island. The Mohawk River, isolated as it was
from the Hudson by the formidable Cohoes Falls, supported

far fewer species and none of the anadromous fish he mentions, such as sturgeon, salmon, or shad.

102. *Twalift* is a spelling pronunciation of the Dutch *twaalf*, "twelve," with the addition of a *t* to mimic the shape of *elft* in order to create a wordplay in the numbering system. The Dutch word for shad, *elft*, is similar to *elf*, "eleven." The wordplay continues with *twalift* and *dertienen*, "thirteens," names given fish with which the Dutch were unfamiliar. See De Vries in Jameson, *Narratives*, 222–23, for a similar discussion.

103. Carp, an Asian fish, were introduced into New York state waters via Europe in the 1830s. By the end of the century they had spread throughout New England. The species called "silverfish" is unknown and may simply represent a description. *Aal* is Dutch for young eel, *paling* for adult eel. The meaning of *brikken* is unknown.

104. Described is the tomcod, also known as the frostfish.

105. See De Vries in Jameson, *Narratives*, 223: "There is a species of fish . . . called by us stone-bream, and by the English *schip-heet*, that is to say, *sheep's head*, for the reason that its mouth is full of teeth, above and below, like a sheep's head."

106. The first two figures are exaggerations.

107. *Sewant*: also known as wampum; small, cylindrical beads made from the whelk (*Buccinum undatum*) and the hard-shell, or quahog, clam (*Venus mercenaria*).

108. This might be a reference to Indian tobacco (*Lobelia inflata*). Eating the roots of this plant in quantity can be fatal.

109. The northern water snake.

110. Van der Donck is describing the timber rattlesnake.

111. Possibly broom snakeweed (*Gutierrezia sarothrae*).

112. This story is doubtful.

113. Juvenile northern coal skinks and five-lined skinks have blue tails.

114. Galen: a reference to Claudius Galenus of Pergamum, the celebrated second-century Greek physician.

115. On population loss resulting from epidemics in the seventeenth century, see Dean R. Snow, "Mohawk Demography and the

Effects of Exogenous Epidemics on American Indian Populations," *Journal of Anthropological Archaeology* 15 (1996): 160–82; Dean R. Snow and Kim Lanphear, "European Contact and Indian Depopulation in the Northeast: The Timing of the First Epidemics," *Ethnohistory* 35 (1988): 15–33.

Of the Original Natives of New Netherland

1. The patron saint of epileptics. The allusion here is obvious.
2. Small beer: a weak beer.
3. *Sappaen*: a variant of *samp*, from Narragansett, *nasaump*. The Mohawk equivalent is *onòn:tara'*.
4. Turkish beans: pole beans.
5. The anadromous rockfish, also known as the striped bass, is not found in the Mohawk River, which suggests that Van der Donck was describing foods of Indians in the Hudson Valley.
6. The elements of dress derived from whales point to Indians from Long Island or southern New England.
7. Modern Munsee has *akootay*, "skirt, petticoat." Ives Goddard, personal communication, January 9, 2006. *Cote* plainly suggests breechclout.
8. *Clootlap*: "balls cover."
9. In 1644 Megapolensis reports of the Indians, "They make themselves stockings and also shoes of deer skin, or they take leaves of their corn, and plait them together and use them for shoes." Jameson, *Narratives*, 173.
10. This suggests pendants or perhaps necklaces of *sewant*.
11. In describing Indian people, Megapolensis wrote, "They all have black hair and eyes, but their skin is yellow." Jameson, *Narratives*, 173.
12. The somewhat incomplete picture of hair hanging over the chest presented here was more fully rendered by Van der Donck in the earlier *Representation*. There, in writing of men's hair styles, he observed that they also wore "other fine hair of the same [red] color, which [hung] around the neck in braids, whereof they [were] very vain." O'Callaghan, *Documents Relative*, 1:281–82. See "The Country," note 67.

13. Seventeenth-century longhouses of the Mohawks and other Iroquoians were, in fact, constructed with interior partitions that set off storage areas at the ends of houses and also living compartments down each side. Archaeological information on the houses of Mahicans, and Munsee-speakers of the lower Hudson Valley, greater New York, western Long Island, and northern New Jersey, is not as plentiful. They were, however, generally smaller in every dimension than their Iroquoian counterparts and, from all indications, lacked interior partitions. Oval or rectangular in form, most were home to one, two, or sometimes several families.

14. Described is an opening running along the "peak" of the house from which smoke could escape.

15. Van der Donck is describing an Iroquois, that is, a Mohawk village. No comparable settlement types are known for the period for any of the Algonquian-speaking groups in the Hudson Valley. Although he had the opportunity to visit Mohawk villages, which were located beginning some forty miles west of Fort Orange, there are suggestions that his depiction may, in part, have been based on Van den Bogaert's journal of 1634–35, and perhaps the writings of Samuel de Champlain, in the latter case, his description of a palisade. Gehring and Starna, *Journey*; H. P. Biggar, ed., *The Works of Samuel de Champlain*, 6 vols. (Toronto: University of Toronto Press, 1971), 3:122. Also, Van der Donck was acquainted with other Dutchmen familiar with Mohawk communities, notably Arent van Curler, secretary and then commissary of the colony, who had close relations with these Native people. A. J. F. van Laer, trans. and ed., *Van Rensselaer Bowier Manuscripts: Being the Letters of Kiliaen van Rensselaer, 1630–1643, and Other Documents Relating to the Colony of Rensselaerswyck* (Albany NY: University of the State of New York, 1908); Thomas E. Burke Jr., *Mohawk Frontier: The Dutch Community of Schenectady, New York, 1661–1710* (Ithaca NY: Cornell University Press, 1991).

16. Given the mention of especially oysters, Van der Donck is referring here to Indians residing in the lower Hudson Valley or the environs of Manhattan and Long Island.

17. *Buyten de pot pist*: "pisses outside the pot," an idiom suggesting infidelity.
18. *Killetjen*: the diminutive of *kill*, "waterway."
19. Native mortuary practices in the region, as documented by archaeological research, were such that bodies were placed in the ground on their sides and in a flexed position, that is, legs bent at the knees and drawn up to the chest, and arms bent at the elbows, hands near the face.
20. "Name" may suggest a specific ethnic identity, that is, Mohawk, Mahican, Wappinger, or others. Alternatively, it might refer to a clan, a residence and kin group composed of multiple households or lineages. For example, writing in 1644, Megapolensis reported, "The Mohawk Indians are divided into three tribes [read "clans"], which are called *Ochkari, Anaware, Oknaho*, that is, the Bear, the Tortoise and the Wolf." Jameson, *Narratives*, 178.
21. "The devil" is a reference to supernaturals.
22. Van der Donck's description of shamanistic behaviors echoes that of Van den Bogaert and also fits well with those of other seventeenth-century observers. See Gehring and Starna, *Journey*, 10, 17–18; Tooker, *Ethnography*, 91–97; Kathleen J. Bragdon, *Native People of Southern New England, 1500–1650* (Norman OK: University of Oklahoma Press, 1996), 200–216.
23. This description is reminiscent of Iroquoian "eat-all" feasts, thought to be associated with hunting rituals. On the other hand, among northeastern Indians generally, the accepted custom was to eat everything that was available or presented to them with the anticipation of leaner times. See Lafitau, *Customs*, 2:89; Tooker, *Ethnography*, 74.
24. *Wilde menschen*: "savage people."
25. *Sachemaes*: sachem, sometimes sagamore, from Proto-Algonquian, *sa:kima:wa*, "leader." Bragdon, *Native People*, 249n3. The term also came to be applied to Mohawk and other Iroquois leaders; however, Native words for such headmen among the Mohawks are *rakowa:neh*, "he is a great one," and *rahsennowa:neh*, "his name is great." Chiefs of the Iroquois

League were *roya:nehr,* "he is a chief" (Mohawk). William N. Fenton, *The Great Law and the Longhouse: A Political History of the Iroquois Confederacy* (Norman OK: University of Oklahoma Press, 1998), 199.

26. The Mohawks, "Sinnekes" (Sinnekens), and Susquehannocks listed here were Iroquoian speakers; the Shawnees, Algonquian speakers; the Manhattans/Rechgawawanks and Wappingers each spoke a Munsee dialect of Eastern Algonquian.

27. Much of Van der Donck's discussion on Indian languages appears to have been drawn from Megapolensis. Jameson, *Narratives,* 172–73.

28. The best discussion on *sewant,* or wampum, is in Fenton, *Great Law,* 224–39.

29. Indians were capable of delivering invectives in their own languages in ways the Dutch might not have understood.

30. In 1628 De Rasieres wrote, "They are very fond of a game they called *Seneca,* played with some round rushes, similar to the Spanish feather-grass, which they understand how to shuffle and deal as though they were playing with cards." Jameson, *Narratives,* 106. Indians in southeastern New England played what appears to have been an identical game, "not much unlike cards and dice, being no other than lottery," called puim. Fifty or sixty small rushes about a foot long, divided among the players, were rolled and shuffled between the palms and then counted. Iroquoians, in turn, used "little white reeds about ten inches long, the size of stems of wheat." Wood, *New England's Prospect,* 103–4; Roger Williams, *A Key into the Language of America* (1643; repr., Providence RI: Roger Williams Press, 1936), 177; Sagard[-Théodat], *Long Journey,* 96–97; Lafitau, *Customs,* 2:195–96.

31. *Stooven:* Dutch, "stoves." The reference is to sweat houses, used by Native people throughout the Northeast.

32. Writing in 1634 and 1635, Van den Bogaert described in some detail curing rituals among the Mohawks and the Oneidas. Gehring and Starna, *Journey,* 10, 17–18.

33. The Indians' tobacco was *Nicotiana rusticum,* not the sweet *N. tobacum.*

34. Van der Donck's depiction of the communal deer hunt and game trap was in all likelihood drawn directly from Champlain. Biggar, *Works*, 3:60–61, 83–85, plate 5. So too was the more detailed description David de Vries published at about the same time as Van der Donck (1655). Jameson, *Narratives*, 218.

35. Rondaxkes: "Adirondacks," from *atirú:taks*, literally "tree eaters," the Mohawk name for the Algonquins, several related Native groups residing in and east of the Ottawa Valley.

36. *Manitou* is an Algonquian word used to express power—natural and supernatural, positive and negative—or the cultivation of power and, more broadly, to suggest tutelary spirits who embody such power. Writing in 1633, Johannes de Laet accurately analogized *Menutto*, *Menetto*, and *Menetto* with *Oqui*, a word, he said, "the Canadians" used. More precisely, *Oqui*, or *oki*, was a Huron word and concept. Nevertheless, De Laet's information on this subject was not firsthand; he had come by it from reading Champlain, who in 1616 had written, "They [the Hurons] have certain persons, who are the *oqui*, or, as the Algonquins and Montagnais call them, *manitous*." Supporting this contention is Champlains's spelling, *oqui*, which appears nowhere else in the literature. Jameson, *Narratives*, 57; Tooker, *Ethnography*, 78, 92; Biggar, *Works*, 3:143.

37. Van der Donck's information on this particular detail of alleged Native political process may have come from Roger Williams, who, writing of Indian government in New England in 1643, reported, "The most usual Custome amongst them in executing punishments, is for the *Sachim* either to beat, or whip, or put to death with his owne hand, to which the common sort most quietly submit: though sometimes the *Sachim* sends a secret Executioner, one of his chiefest Warriours to fetch of a head, by some sudden unexpected blow of a Hatchet, when they have feared Mutiny by publike execution." See Williams, *Key into the Language*, 136.

38. Kintowen: Munsee, *kúndüween*, "Sunday." See John O'Meara, *Delaware–English/English–Delaware Dictionary* (Toronto: University of Toronto Press, 1996), 108. Apparently there was a verb

*kúndüweew, "he prays, worships in the Christian fashion," but this is unattested. *Kúndüween* would once have been "people (indefinite) pray (in whatever way this is)." Ives Goddard, personal communication, December 11, 2005.

39. The tenor of this discussion on religion echoes what Johannes Megapolensis had provided in 1644. See Jameson, *Narratives*, 177–78.

40. Similar sentiments were expressed by the Reverend Jonas Michaëlius in 1628. Jameson, *Narratives*, 128–29.

41. Beliefs in the afterlife varied among Indian people; however, among northern Iroquoians one of the two souls of a deceased person was believed to travel to a village in the west. Tooker, *Ethnography*, 140. Wassenaer reported that a Mahican soul "goes up westward on leaving the body." Jameson, *Narratives*, 86.

42. See Megapolensis's discussion in Jameson, *Narratives*, 177.

43. A number of the opening elements of the cosmological myth that Van der Donck recounts are common to those found among both Northern Iroquoians and Eastern Algonquians. Compare the Mohawk version reported by Megapolensis in 1644. Jameson, *Narratives*, 178. However, the motif of the pregnant sky woman giving birth to a deer, a bear, a wolf, and, sometime afterward, a diversity and multitude of offspring fathered by these animals, does not appear in any of the well-documented Iroquoian creation stories; that is, it is not of Iroquoian origin. But neither does it conform to the one or two versions recorded for Munsee speakers of the lower Hudson Valley, northern New Jersey, Manhattan, and western Long Island. Nothing is known of Mahican creation stories. Nonetheless, Van der Donck's account most likely came from an Algonquian-speaking group. See William N. Fenton, "This Island, the World on the Turtle's Back," *Journal of American Folklore* 75 (1962): 283–300; also Fenton, *Great Law*, 34–50; William W. Newcomb Jr., *The Culture and Acculturation of the Delaware Indians*, University of Michigan Museum of Anthropology, Anthropological Papers 10 (1956; repr., Ann Arbor: University of Michigan, 1970), 71–73.

44. A reference to Virgil's epic poem *Aeneid*, considered a greatly improved literary history of the founding of Rome from that told by Quintus Ennius in his *Annales*.

Of the Nature of the Beavers

1. Van der Donck errs. The correct citation is book 32, chapter 13. [Pliny the Elder,] *Natural History*, 6:13–15.
2. Olaus Magnus (1490–1558), Swedish geographer, naturalist, and prelate, and Albertus Magnus (1193 or 1206–80) from Swabia, scholastic philosopher and also a naturalist.
3. Podagra is gout specific to the joints of the foot or the great toe.
4. The actual etymologies are *kastoras* in Greek and both *fiber* and *castor* in Latin.
5. Osier: also known as basket willow (*Salix viminalis*), introduced into North America by Europeans.
6. There are several possibilities for the identity of Sextus: Sextus Iulius Africanus (c. 160–240), who wrote *Kestoi* (Embroiderings), which in part dealt with veterinary practices and medicine; Sextus Empiricus (2nd–3rd centuries), physician and philosopher who was also interested in the natural history of animals; and Sextus Placitus (5th century), the author of a treatise on the medicinal use of animals.
7. A number of the characteristics that Van der Donck attributes to the beaver are plainly fanciful—for example, that their lodges were built with four and five stories and that female beavers carried lengths of cut trees on their backs assisted by their mates and progeny.
8. Female beavers have four teats.
9. Georgius Agricola, a.k.a. Georg Bauer (1494–1555), from Saxony, widely regarded as the founder of the science of mineralogy, was also a student of natural history.
10. These "glands" were the beaver's kidneys.
11. Castoreum is produced by scent glands located in the cloaca of both male and female beavers, which waterproof their fur by coating it with this oily substance. Castoreum also functions for

these animals as a sexual attractant and has long been believed to have medicinal qualities for humans.

A Conversation

1. "The war" is a reference to the first Anglo-Dutch War, 1652–54.
2. A reference to a war with Indians on the Manhattan rim, 1643–45, often called Kieft's War.
3. A reference to the Peace of Westphalia in 1648, ending the Eighty Years' War.

INDEX

grapes, 25–28
Groot, Hugo de, xi, xiii

Halve Maen, 1–2, 3, 10
hares, 52
Heermans, Augustijn, 153n41
hemp, 38
herbs, medicinal, 32–33
hickory trees, 20, 21
hogs, 45–46, 68
Hooghes, Anthony de, 149n11
hornbeams, 23
horses, 44
Hudson, Henry, x, 2
Hudson River, 5, 10–13

Indians: agriculture by, 97–98;
arrival of, in New World,
92–93; and beans, 31; and
bears, 48–49; and beavers,
119, 124–25, 126, 140;
and birds, 55; and chest-
nuts, 23, 78; and child-
birth, 84–87; children of,
87–88; and Christianity,
106–8, 110–11; clothing
of, 78–81, 119; death customs of, 88–90; encounters
of, with colonists, xi, 3–4,
39, 103–4, 134–36, 148n4;
and fish, 98–99; and food,
76–78, 123, 165n23; and
gifts, 104–5; government of,
93, 105–6; and health care,
96–97; houses of, 81–82, 83,
164n13, 164n15; hunting by,
47–50, 68–69, 98–99, 119,
124, 159n73; justice system
of, 102–3, 167n37; languages of, 93–94; mannerisms
of, 95–96; and marriage,
84–87, 93; and minerals,
39–40; and money, 94–95;
names of groups of, 150n16;
paints and dyes used by,
41–43; pastimes of, 96,
166n30; physical characteristics of, 73–76; and pumpkins, 29; religious beliefs
of, 106–8, 109–14, 168n41,
168n43; and snakes, 60–62;
social classes of, 100; special gatherings of, 90–91,
165n23; and universal law
of nations, 103–4; and warfare, xi, 39, 100–101; water
travel by, 12, 13, 16, 150n17;
weapons of, 101, 157n66. *See
also* settlements, Indian
indigo, 32–33

Jogues, Isaac, 159n75
Johnson, Jeremiah, xvii–xix

Kats Kil. *See* Catskill Creek
Kieft, Willem, xi, xii, 39, 40,
53, 126, 154n53, 155n59
Kil van Col, 8
Kintowen, 107, 167n38

Lake of the Iroquois, 12
La Montagne, Johannes, 40,
154n57

lizards, 62
lobsters, 59
Long Island, 7, 9, 14, 133–34

madder root, 33
Magellan, Ferdinand, 92
Magnus, Albertus, 116, 119,
    120, 121, 124, 169n2
Magnus, Olaus, 116, 119, 120,
    121, 124, 169n2
Manhattan Island, 11
Maquas-kil. *See* Mohawk
    River
Mauritius River, 4
medicine, 32–33, 96–97,
    115–16, 124–26, 169n11
Megapolensis, Johannis, 36,
    154n47
melons, 29–30
minerals, 38–41, 95, 156n60
minks, 52
Minuit, Peter, 147n3, 153n42
Mohawk River, 12
moose, 159n72
Morison, Samuel Eliot, x
murder, 102–3

Navesink River, 8
New Amsterdam, xvi, 9, 11, 14
Newesinck. *See* Navesink River
New Jersey, 154n54
New Netherland: Adriaen van
    der Donck's arrival in, xi;
    animals of, 44–53, 54–56,
    57–58, 60–62, 92–93,
    149n11, 158n68, 158n71,

159n72, 161n101; boundar-
ies of, 5–6; coast of, 5–9,
132–33; discovery of, x,
1–2; Dutch control of, xiii–
xiv, 4–5, 149n7, 154n49;
European migration to, xv,
127–42; flowers of, 31–32;
foreshore of, 6–9; land characteristics of, 17–19, 38–41;
location of, 1; naming of,
2–4; rivers of, 9–15; seaports
of, 6–9; strategic advantages
of settling of, 127–42; trade
in, 33, 128, 137–42, 147n2;
trees of, 19–25, 128; vegetables of, 28–31; vegetation of,
19–24; vineyards of, 25–28;
weather of, 2–3, 62–71;
wetlands of, 18–19. *See also*
settlers, New Netherland
New Sweden, 3
New York, xvi
North River, 5, 10–13
nut trees, 23, 24, 152n28

oak trees, 21, 24
O'Donnell, Thomas, ix
Of Plymouth Plantation
    (Bradford), x
oxen, 45, 68

paints, 41–43, 157n62
partridges, 54–55
Pauw, Michael, 154n50
peas, 34–35
Pelen, Brandt, 36, 154n49

CPSIA information can be obtained at www.ICGtesting.com
Printed in the USA
LVOW08s1638301213

367456LV00002B/309/P

9 780803 232839